Das ultimative Probenbuch
ENGLISCH

Gymnasium E1/E2 2.Jahr

This book belongs to

____

Vorwort

Liebe Schülerin, lieber Schüler,

dieses Buch hilft dir beim Lernen, sowie bei der Vorbereitung auf deine Schulaufgaben bzw. Stegreifaufgaben im zweiten Englischjahr. Zu Beginn fassen wir den gesamten Grammatikstoff kurz zusammen und geben dir ein paar nützliche Tipps. Wir versuchen das gesamte Buch möglichst auf Englisch zu halten, damit du dich an die Sprache gewöhnst.

Damit du wirklich alles verstehen kannst, haben wir schwere Passagen auch auf Deutsch formuliert. Lese bitte immer erst den englischen Text und versuche dabei selbst zu erkennen wie viel du wirklich verstehst. Am Anfang findest du mehr deutsche Hinweise, zum Ende des Buches werden diese immer weniger. Wir haben den deutschen Text farblich grau abgesetzt.

Anhand der von uns erstellten Proben, die dem Lehrplan angepasst sind und in Inhalt, Form und Umfang etwa dem entsprechen, was dich in deinen Klassenarbeiten erwartet, kannst du überprüfen, ob du den behandelten Stoff beherrschst. In der Regel hast du für eine Schulaufgabe 45 Minuten Zeit.

Im Anhang findest du zu jeder Probe eine Lösung mit ausführlichen Antworten, damit du deine Proben selbstständig kontrollieren kannst.

Wir wünschen dir viel Erfolg bei der Arbeit mit dieser Probensammlung und für dein Schuljahr.

Mandana Mandl Joscelin Peyman

Für konstruktive Kritik und Tipps, wie auch für Ideen für weitere Schulproben sind wir immer offen!

1. Auflage 9/2014

Lektorat: Prof. Dr. Peter Mandl, Sylvia Field

www.Mandl-Verlag.de

FSC
www.fsc.org
MIX
Papier aus verantwortungsvollen Quellen
FSC® C008457

Informatives:

In dieser Reihe erhältlich:

3. Klasse:	Deutsch, Mathematik, Heimat – und Sachunterricht (HSU)
3./4. Klasse:	Deutsch – Leseprobenbuch
4. Klasse:	Deutsch, Mathematik, Heimat – und Sachunterricht (HSU)
5: Klasse	Deutsch, Mathematik, Englisch - Gymnasium, **neu Englisch Realschule**
6. Klasse:	Deutsch, Mathematik, **neu Englisch - Gymnasium**

Ferienkalender für Bayern:

	2014	**2015**
Fasching	03.03. – 07.03.	16.02. – 20.02
Ostern	14.04. – 26.04.	30.03. – 11.04
Pfingsten	10.06. – 21.06.	26.05. – 05.06
Sommer	30.07. – 15.09.	01.08. – 14.09
Herbst	27.10. – 31.10.	02.11. – 07.11.
Weihnachten	24.12. – 05.01.	24.12. – 05.01.

Ferienkalender für Baden – Württemberg:

	2014	**2015**
Ostern	14.04. – 25.04.	30.03. – 10.04.
Pfingsten	10.06. – 21.06	26.05. – 06.06.
Sommer	31.07. – 13.09.	30.07. – 12.09.
Herbst	27.10. – 30.10.	02.11. – 06.11.
Weihnachten	22.12. – 05.01.	23.12. – 09.01.

Quelle: http://www.schulferien.org

Content

1 Grammar Summary

1.1 Question Tags

1.1.1 Question Tags – Form and Function

Question tags are often used in spoken English. We put a question tag on the end of a sentence when we want **confirmation** *(Bestätigung)* **or agreement** *(Zustimmung)*. It is a 'mini question'.

A **question tag** is usually formed using an **auxiliary verb.** An **auxiliary verb** is not the main verb in your sentence but the **'helping verb'.** (If the verb 'to be' is your main verb, then you use it to form the question tag.)

If the **sentence is positive → the question tag is negative** and if **the sentence is negative → the question tag is positive.**

Last but not least **don't forget the comma**.

*In unserem ersten Kapitel stellen wir dir eine Besonderheit des **gesprochenen Englisch** vor: die sogenannten „**question tags**". Hier handelt es sich im Englischen um Hilfsverben als kleine Anhängsel, die ans Satzende angehängt werden und die man im Deutschen mit: „stimmt's?", "oder?" Bzw. „nicht wahr?" übersetzen könnte. In der Regel gilt:*

- *Ist der Hauptsatz bejaht, wird im Question Tag verneint.*
- *Ist der Hauptsatz verneint, wird im Question Tag bejaht.*

*„**question tags**" werden immer durch ein Komma getrennt.*

Zum besseren Verständnis ein paar Beispiele:

positive →negative	negative → positive
You **have** got a dog, **haven't** you?	Mary **can't** drive, **can** she?
Big Ben **is** in London, **isn't** it?	We **weren't** late, **were** we?
Christine **is** coming home, **isn't** she?	She **hasn't** got a cold, **has** she?
They **must** pay for the coffee, **mustn't** they?	We **aren't** going to visit Australia, **are** we?

Note

We don't use names or nouns in the question tags, we use the **subject pronouns**. We also use **short forms** where possible.

*Im ‚question tag' wird kein Nomen oder Name verwendet, sondern das entsprechende Pronomen und das Verb in **short form**.*

Stuart isn't going to eat all the cake, is **he**? → 'he' → **not** 'Stuart'
The children are playing in the park, **aren'**t they? → **not** 'are not' they.
Munich is in Bavaria, **isn't** it. → **not** 'is not it'.

It is important that you know the **short forms.** Compare the two examples below.

She**'s** at school, **isn't** she? → **'s** stands for 'is'
She**'s** got a school bag, **hasn't** she? → **'s** stands for 'has'

'he she it – das 's' muss mit

1.1.2 Question Tags in Simple Present and Simple Past

When we have a sentence in the **simple present positive** or **simple past positive** we can't see the auxiliary verb, it is hidden. We need it to form the question tag.
In diesen Sätzen kannst du das Hilfsverb nicht immer sehen, dennoch brauchst du es, um ein question tag zu formulieren.

The auxiliary verbs for the **simple present** are either '**do**' or '**does**'.

simple present positive → negative	simple present negative → positive
Rebecca **spends** Christmas at home, **doesn't** she?	Rebecca **doesn't** spend Christmas at home, **does** she?
Prince Charles **lives** in London, **doesn't** he?	Prince Charles **doesn't live** in London, **does he**?
You **eat** meat, **don't** you?	You **don't eat** meat, **do** you?
They **study** hard, **don't they**?	They **don't study** hard, **do** they?

The auxiliary verb for the **simple past** is '**did**'.

simple past positive →negative	simple past negative → positive
Michael **won** the race, **didn't** he?	Michael **didn't win** the race, **did he**?
Robin Hood **helped** rich people, **didn't** he?	Robin Hood **didn't help** rich people, **did** he?
She **sent** the text**, didn't** she?	She **didn't send** the text, **did** she?

1.1.3 Intonation (*Betonung*)

It is fun practising the intonation when you use question tags.

Your voice goes down when you expect your partner to **agree** with what you are saying *(Stimme wird tiefer, wenn man Zustimmung erwartet).* You know that what you are saying is probably correct. It is a way to bring your partner into the conversation.

Examples

We always get a lot of homework, don't we?

London isn't in Scotland, is it?

If we are **unsure** and possibly need more **information**, our voices go up. *(Stimme wird höher, wenn wir uns nicht sicher sind)*

Examples

We have two weeks holiday at Christmas, don't we?

We aren't going to have a test on Friday, are we?

Exercise 1

Fill in the correct question tags.

1. *Anna was late, __________________?*
2. *You didn't need your pen, __________________?*
3. *He must be on time, __________________?*
4. *We can't telephone all the children, __________________?*
5. *Mobile phones cost a lot of money, __________________?*
6. *The teacher told us the answer, __________________?*

1.2 Adjectives

An adjective is a word that describes a noun or pronoun. Adjectives can also be used to describe actions that are the subject of a sentence.

Examples

The **blue** car.

I saw an **angry old** man.

It is **sunny.**

Drinking iced water in the summer is **refreshing**.

1.2.1 Comparatives

We use adjectives when we want to compare things or people. *(Adjektive zum Vergleichen)*

Comparatives compare two people or things.

'than' not 'th**e**n"

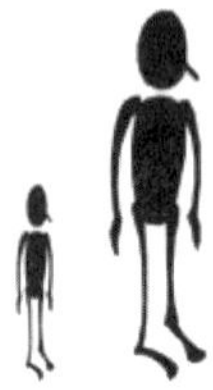

Tony is **taller than** John. - *Tony ist größer als John*

John - Tony

£10,000

Ring A

£500

Ring B

Ring A is **more expensive than** ring B.

Follow the **rules** when making sentences using **comparatives**.

1. The comparative is always followed by **'than'.**
2. **'er'** is added to a **one syllable** (***einsilbig***) adjective.

   Examples: A Ferrari is **faster than** a Polo. (fast → faster)
   An apple is **smaller than** a melon. (small → smaller)

   Spelling

   If the adjective ends in 'e' just add 'r'. (lat**e**-late**r**, nic**e**-nice**r**)
   If the last letter of the adjective is a single consonant, double the consonant.
   (big - bi**gg**er, fa**t** - fa**tt**er)

3. We use '**more + adjective**' for adjectives which have **three or more syllables**. (interesting, beautiful, important).

   Examples: A Ferrari is **more expensive than** a Polo**.**
   A horror film is **more frightening than** a science fiction film.

4. Adjectives that have **two syllables** form the comparative with either **'er'** or **'more'.** Please see the table below.

Adjectives with two syllables which use **'er'** to form the comparative.	Examples
Adjectives ending in 'y' - (the 'y' changes to 'i' then add 'er')	His dog is **sillier than** my dog. (silly) My new dress is **prettier than** old dress. (pretty)
Adjectives ending in 'er'	Jack is **cleverer than** Tom. (clever)
Adjectives ending in 'le'.	A children's book is **simpler than** an adult's book. (simple)
Adjectives with two syllables which use 'more' to form the comparative.	**Examples**
Most two syllable adjectives especially adjectives ending in 'ful', 'ious', 'ed' , 'ous', 'ing'	My teacher is **more helpful than** my friend. (helpful) Madonna is **more famous than** Sarah Connor. (famous) Doing nothing is **more boring than** watching TV. (boring)

Please note that these rules for two syllable adjectives are a guide. It is important that the students follow their teacher's suggestions when answering questions on a test.

Exercise 2

Fill in the spaces with the correct comparative form.

1. *Going to the cinema is ___________________ (cheap) going to the theatre.*
2. *My dad is ______________________ (serious) my mum.*
3. *A park is ___________________ (peaceful) than a disco.*
4. *His swimming pool is ____________________ (large) my swimming pool.*
5. *The test was _________________________ (difficult) the quiz.*
6. *Maria is ___________________________ (happy) than Jenny.*

1.2.2 Superlatives

Superlatives compare one person or thing with a group.

The Tower of London is one of <u>**the**</u> **oldest** buildings in England.

£95,000

This is <u>**the**</u> **most expensive** ring in the shop.

Follow these **rules** when making sentences using **superlatives.**

1. Write '<u>**the**</u>' in front of the superlative. (<u>**the**</u> biggest, <u>**the**</u> most beautiful)
2. '**est**' is added to one syllable adjectives. (sad, quick, nice)

   Examples: I ate <u>**the**</u> **biggest** cake in the shop.
   She is <u>**the**</u> **shortest** girl in the class.

   Spelling
   If the adjective ends in 'e' just add 'st'. (lat**e**→lat**est**, nic**e**→nic**est**)
   If the last letter is a single consonant, double the consonant.
   (bi**g**-bi**gg**est, fa**t**-fa**tt**est)

3. We use '**the most** + **adjective**' for adjectives that have **three or more syllables**. (exciting, delicious, intelligent)

   Examples: He is **the most serious** boy in the class.
   It is **the most interesting** book in the library.

4. Adjectives which have **two syllables** form the superlative with either '**est**' or '**most**'. (Please see the table below.)

Adjectives with two syllables which use **'est'** to form the **superlative**.	Examples
Adjectives ending in 'y' - (the 'y' changes to 'i' then add 'est')	It was **the easiest** test last year. (easy) She has got **the tidiest** desk in the classroom. (tidy)
Adjectives ending in 'er' or le'	It was **the simplest** question on the test. (simple)

Adjectives with two syllables which use **'most'** to form the **superlative**.	Examples
Most two syllable adjectives especially adjectives ending in 'ful', 'ious', 'ed' , 'ous', ing	It was **the most useful** book I have ever bought. (useful) She is **the most anxious** person I have ever met. (anxious)

Please note that these rules for two syllable adjectives are a guide. It is important that the students follow their teacher's suggestions when answering questions on a test.

Exercise 3

Fill in the correct superlative form.

1. *It was _____________ (sad) film I have ever seen.*
2. *He is ___________________ (thoughtful-fürsorglich) teacher in the school.*
3. *It was ___________________ (busy) day of my life.*
4. *It was ___________________ (cold) day of the year.*
5. *She is ___________________ (generous) woman in the world.*
6. *She is ___________________ (friendly) girl in the class.*

1.2.3 Irregular Comparatives and Superlatives

Some comparatives and superlatives are **irregular** and do not follow the rules. Unfortunately you just have to learn them, there are no tricks. It is important that you learn them because they are words that we always use.

adjective	irregular comparative	irregular superlative
good	better	best
bad	worse	worst
little (quantity)	less	least
much	more	most
far*	farther	farthest
	further	furthest

*farther, further, farthest and furthest can all be used to describe distances

Berlin is **farther/ furthest** from Munich **than** Frankfurt.

Further, furthest can also be used in an abstract sense to mean 'additional'

I am **further** in the book **than** John.

Exercise 4

Fill in the correct form of the adjective.

1. *My best friend is_________ at dancing _________ I am.(good)*
2. *I need ___________time to finish the homework __________you do.(much)*
3. *It was ________________day of his life.(bad)*
4. *She is _________________ teacher in the whole world.(good)*

1.2.4 As.....as /not as......as

We can also make comparisons using '**as......as**' or '**not as.......as**'.

Look at the following examples

- A hamster is **as small as** a mouse. (both a hamster and a mouse are small)

- A rat is **not as small as** a mouse. (both are small but a rat is still bigger than a mouse)

- Cycling is **as fun as** motorcycling. (both are fun)
- Cycling **isn't as fast as** motorcycling. (both are fast but riding a motorbike is faster)

The **(not) as.......as** is formed using an adjective.

(not) as + adjective + as

Paul is **as tall as** his uncle.

You are **as clever as** your best friend.

A chair isn't **as comfortable as** a sofa.

His boots aren't **as dirty as** my boots.

Be careful:
In these sentences 'as" does not mean 'als'. It means 'wie'.

Exercise 5

Fill in the spaces using the correct adjective.

1. *Her dress is ________________________________ (**so schön wie)** her sister's dress.*
2. *The film was ________________________________ (**nicht so spannend wie**) the book.*
3. *My new computer is __________________________ (**nicht so gut wie**) my old computer.*
4. *Her new song is ______________________________ (**nicht so beliebt wie**) her old song.*
5. *My new teacher is ____________________________ (**so nett wie**) my old teacher.*
6. *Learning vocabulary is ________________________ (**so wichtig wie**) learning grammar.*

1.2.5 Translation of comparative sentences

There are **few false friends** when translating German sentences into English sentences. This could cost you a few points on a test. Make sure you know the 'little' words.

→ **Achte auf die 'false friends' um hier nicht unnötig Punkte zu verschenken!**

- Er ist größer **als** sein Bruder.
  He is bigger **than** his brother. (not 'as')

- Er ist nicht **so** groß **wie** seine Schwester.
  He is not **as** tall **as** his sister. (not 'so')

Exercise 6

Please translate the sentences.

1. Das blaue Buch ist wichtiger als das rote Buch.

____

2. Wir sind (genau)so schlau wie die andere Klasse.

____

1.3 Adverbs of Manner – modale Adverbien

An **adverb adds information to a verb**. Adverbs can add information saying **how**, **when** or **where** something is done.

We will focus on **'how'** an adverb modifies a verb. These types of adverbs are called **adverbs of manner** **(Adverb der Art und Weise)**.

1.3.1 Adverbs - Form

An **adverb of manner** is formed by adding **'ly' to the adjective**.

adjective	adverb
slow	slow**ly**
sweet	sweet**ly**
bad	bad**ly**
sudden	sudden**ly**
clear	clear**ly**
quick	quick**ly**
warm	warm**ly**

In the winter we must **dress warmly**.

There are a few spelling rules that we have to learn when we add the 'ly'.

If the adjective ends in a **consonant plus 'le'**, **drop** the **'e'** and add **'y'**.

simp**le**	simp**ly**
gent**le**	gent**ly**
responsib**le**	responsib**ly**

If the adjectives ends in **'y'**, change the **'y'** to **'i'** and add **'ly'**.

eas**y**	eas**ily**
angr**y**	angr**ily**
happ**y**	happ**ily**
luck**y**	luck**ily**

If the adjective ends in **'ic'** add **'ally'**.

fantast**ic**	fantast**ically**
dramat**ic**	dramat**ically**
bas**ic**	bas**ically**

There are **a few irregular adverbs** of manner that do not follow the rules.

Irregular adverbs of manner

good	well
hard	hard
fast	fast
long	long
high	high

Achtung:
hard = schwer
'hardly' = 'kaum'

Exercise 7

Change the following adjectives to adverbs

busy ________________

hard ________________

terrible ________________

brave (tapfer/mutig) ________________

energetic ________________

1.3.2 Adverbs - Function

An **adjective** describes a **person or thing** and an **adverb** of manner describes **how we do something** (the verb). → Ein Adjektiv beschreibt ein Nomen oder eine Person näher, das Adverb beschreibt das Verb näher, die Art und Weise wie etwas getan wird)

Look at the examples

My car is slow. ('slow' describes the car)

I drive slowly. ('slow' describes how I drive)

The book is good. ('good' describes the book)

She reads well. ('well' describes how she reads)

We saw an **excellent film** at the cinema.

The actor **played** the role **excellently.**

The **children** were **quiet.**

The children **came into** the room **quietly.**

Exceptions/Ausnahmen

We do **not** use adverbs with verbs that describe our **senses**.

to look - to taste - to feel - to smell - (to sound)

Examples:

You **look <u>great</u>**!
I **felt <u>bad</u>** when I heard the news.
Your perfume **smells <u>wonderful</u>**.
The roast beef **tastes <u>delicious</u>**.
Your idea **sounds <u>excellent</u>**.

Be careful!

These verbs **can** also describe an action. If these verbs describe an **action** we use an **adverb**. Please see the examples below.

→ wenn mit diesen Verben eine Aktion beschrieben wird, benutzt man ein Adverb.

Compare: Hier findest du Beispiele mit Adverbien und Adjektiven verwendet.

The fizzy drink **tasted sweet**. (senses→ adjective)
→ (Das sprudelnde Getränk) Die Limonade schmeckte süß.

That cake **looks delicious**. (senses→ adjective)
→ Dieser Kuchen sieht köstlich aus.

I **looked closely** at the class photo but I couldn't see you in it. (action → adverb)
→ Ich habe das Klassenfoto ganz genau angesehen, aber ich konnte dich darauf nicht finden.

I **feel bad** about the lies. (senses→ adjective)
→ Ich fühle mich schlecht wegen der Lüge

I **felt** the cat's injured leg very **carefully**. (action → adverb)
→Ich tastete das verletzte Bein der Katze sehr vorsichtig ab.

Rotten meat **smells disgusting**. (senses →adjective)
→ Verdorbenes Fleisch riecht ecklig.

We always **smell** the meat **properly** to make sure it is fresh. (action →adverb)
→ Wir riechen immer sorgfältig am Fleisch um sicherzustellen, dass es frisch ist.

We also use adjectives with the verbs:

to be, to seem, to become, to get, to stay, to remain

Position of adverbs of manner

Adverbs of manner are **usually** placed directly after the main verb or its direct object.

Examples

The children **sang beautifully**.

The dog **ate its food greedily** (gierig).

We **did our homework enthusiastically**.

The builders **must build the house correctly**.

Exercise 8

Choose the correct form. Adjective or adverb?

1. *I have got a fantastic/fantastically new computer.*

2. *The ballet dancer danced beautiful/beautifully.*

3. *The dinner smells wonderful/wonderfully.*

4. *The dog lay lazy/lazily under the tree.*

5. *The train journey was really bad/badly.*

6. *The team played good/well.*

7. *The teacher became angry/angrily when we didn't stop talking.*

8. *It was raining heavy/heavily so we stayed indoors.*

1.3.3 Adverbs of Manner – Comparatives and Superlatives

The **comparative and superlative** forms of adverbs of manner are normally formed by adding **'more'** or **'most'** to the adverb.

Examples

He works **more quickly** than his father does. (schneller)

Mrs Smith skis **more carefully** than her children do. (vorsichtiger)

He types **more slowly than** his daughter does. (langsamer)

He drives **more dangerously than** his brother does. (gefährlicher)

Exceptions (Ausnahmen)

Adverbs that do not have a different form to the adjective and have one syllable (Silbe) form the comparative and superlative using 'er' or 'est'.

The students **work the hardest** right before the exams. (hard – harder – the hardest)

My dad **drives faster** than my mum. (fast - faster- the fastest)

There are also some irregular comparative and superlative adverbial forms.

adverb	comparative adverb	superlative adverb
well	better	the best
badly	worse	the worst
far	farther/further	the farthest/the furthest*

*far is not by definition an adverb of manner but we thought it would be useful to include it here.

Examples

Sally **plays tennis better than** her partner.
→ Sally spielt besser Tennis als ihre Partnerin.

Our team scored **worse** in the finals than our rivals.
→Unser Team war schlechter im Finale als unsere Konkurrenz / Rivalen.

She **danced the best/worst** in the group.
→ Sie tanzte am besten/schlechtesten in der Klasse/Gruppe.

1.3.4 As.....As Comparisons - Adverbs of Manner

Comparisons (Vergleiche) using **(not) as.......as** are formed using the adverb.

Examples

Mary speaks Chinese **as badly as** her husband does.
→ Mary spricht genauso schlecht chinesisch wie ihr Mann.

This machine does**n't** work **as efficiently as** the old one did.
→ Dieses Gerät läuft **nicht so effizient wie** das alte.

You speak English **as well as** your friends do.
→ Du sprichst **genauso gut** Englisch wie deine Freunde.

My paper airplane flies just **as fast as** your paper airplane does.
Mein Papierflieger fliegt **genauso schnell wie** deiner.

Exercise 9

Fill in the spaces with the correct form of the adverb.

1. *You speak English ____________ (well) this year than you did last year.*
2. *Rebecca runs the ___________ (fast) in the class.*
3. *The children can text _______________ (quickly) than their parents can.*
4. *The bus driver drives the ______________ (carefully) when the school children are on the bus.*
5. *He doesn't write reports (Berichte) as _____________ (clearly) as his colleague (Kollege) does.*
6. *My mum can cook as ___________ (well) as my grandmother can.*

1.4 Past Progressive

1.4.1 Past Progressive - Form

The **past progressive** is formed with 'was/were' plus main verb + 'ing'.

Examples

I **was watching** TV.
The children **were playing** in the park.
We **weren't laughing** at him.
Was Rebecca **listening** to the explanation?
Were you **waiting** for a long time?
Who **were** you **talking** to?
What **was** Nina **doing**?

It is important to remember that some verbs cannot be used in the 'ing form'.

These verbs usually describe a 'state' and not an action. A 'state' is something that exists and can't be 'in progress'.
Denk daran, dass es Wörter gibt, die nicht in die Verlaufsform gesetzt werden dürfen, hierbei handelt es sich meistens um Wörter, die einen Zustand oder ein Gefühl beschreiben.

Examples include:

verbs **not** in the 'ing' form

to know, to understand, to believe, to remember, to forget,
to want, to need, to prefer, to love, to like, to hate, to belong,
to cost, to owe, to recognize, to mean

1.4.2 Past Progressive - Function

The **past progressive** is used in the following situations in English. This tense always implies (*bedeutet*) that the action **was 'in progress'**.

present progressive – function
1. an action in progress in the past interrupted by another action in the past. 2. an action in progress at specific time in the past. 3. two actions in progress at the same time in the past.

1. An action that was **'in progress'** (in Gang sein) but **interrupted** (unterbrochen) by another action. We use the **simple past** for the action that **'interrupts'** the action 'in progress'. It does not matter which part of the sentence comes first.
Past progressive wird verwendet, wenn eine gerade stattfindende Aktion unterbrochen wird. Der Satz mit dem Grund der Unterbrechung steht in simple past.

Examples

- While I **was watching** TV, the telephone **rang**.
- They **were having** dinner when we **arrived.**
- Emily and Hannah **were playing** in the garden when their father **came** home.
- It started to rain while we **were having** a picnic.

Here it is also important to note the **key words** (Schlüssel-/Signalwörter) that are used with the past progressive.

'While' (*während*) is used with the **past progressive** part of the sentence or the action that was 'in progress'.

While the boy **was swimming** in the pool, the dog jumped in the water.
The dog jumped in the pool **while** the boy **was swimming** in the water.

'When' (*als*) is used in the **simple past** part of the sentence or the action that **'Interrupted'** the action that was 'in progress'.

Examples
Annabelle was walking home **when** she **met** Andrew.
When Tina **phoned,** I was having a shower.
The children **were screaming and shouting** when the teacher **came** into the room.

We use the **simple past** when we want to talk about two actions that happened one after the other. (→ zwei aufeinanderfolgende Aktionen)

- When I **saw** the accident, I **phoned** the police. (simple past-simple past)
  *→ **1.** I saw the accident - then → **2.** I phoned the police.)*
- We **started** the lesson when the teacher **arrived**. (simple past- simple past)
  *→ **1.** The teacher arrived - then → **2.** We started the lesson.)*

Comma

A **comma is** used when the **'while' or 'when'** part is at the **beginning of a sentence**.
Ein Komma wird nur gesetzt, wenn der Nebensatz (while,when) am Satzanfang steht.

Compare

We were taking a test **when the fire alarm rang**. (→no comma)
When the fire alarm rang, we were taking a test. (→comma)

While the fire brigade was putting out the fire, the hose broke. (→comma)
The hose broke **while the fire brigade was putting out the fire**. (→no comma)

2. An action that was **'in progress'** at a specific time in the past.
Examples
What **were you doing** at **six o'clock** this morning?
I **was** still **doing** homework **at 10 o'clock** last night.
We **were driving** to London **at lunchtime** yesterday.

3. The past progressive is also used to talk about two actions that were 'in progress' at the same time in the past.
Examples
My mum **was cooking** the dinner while **we were watching** TV.
What **were you doing** while we **were working**?

We often use the past progressive at the beginning of a story. It gives us a picture of what was happening before an event took place.

Example
The sun **was shining** and the children **were playing** in the garden. Mary and John **were playing** football and little Annie **was sitting** on the blanket with her mum. Timmy, their dog, **was sleeping** peacefully under a big leafy tree. Suddenly they **heard** a loud noise. The dog **woke up** and little Annie **screamed**.

Exercise 10

Put the verbs into the correct form. Simple past or past progressive?

1. *We saw an accident while we ____________________ (to stand) at the traffic light.*
2. *It was still raining when the football match ____________________ (to start).*
3. *I ____________________ (to do) my homework at seven o'clock last night.*
4. *I ____________________ (to drive) while he was sleeping.*
5. *I had a cup of tea when I_______________ (to get up).*
6. *What was the teacher doing when you _______________ (to come) into the classroom?*

1.5 Present Perfect

The present perfect is used to talk about actions that have taken place in the past. It is important (wichtig) that you understand when to use the present perfect and when to use the simple past. There are also quite a few irregular verbs which you have to learn.

1.5.1 Present Perfect- Form

Positive

The present perfect is formed with the verb '**to have**' and the **past participle** of the **main verb.**

subject	verb	object(s)	place/time
Rebecca	has eaten	all the cake.	
Our teachers	have given	us a lot of homework.	
I	have seen	Lucy	this week.
The dog	has drunk	its water.	

Don´t forget '**he, she** and **it**' takes **'has'**.

Negative

The **negative** is formed by adding the word **'not' after 'have'or 'has'**.

subject	verb	object/ place/time
My children	have not done (haven't done)	their homework.
The president	has not seen (hasn't seen)	the report.
We	have not broken (haven't broken)	the photocopier.
Our class	has not been (hasn't been)	on a field trip (Ausflug)this year.

Questions

Questions are formed by **<u>switching</u> the subject and 'have' or 'has'**.

I have never written a letter in English.

Have you ever written a letter in English?

The students have cooked their teacher a meal.

Have the students cooked their teacher a meal.

Exercise 11

Put in the correct form of the present perfect.

1. *______ your son ____________________ (to copy) the homework?*
2. *John ____________________ (to be) at work all day.*
3. *Gill and Ken _____________ just _______________ (to clean) the house.*
4. *I _____________________ (to eat/not) anything so far.*

1.5.2 Present Perfect - Function

It is easy to form the present perfect but you have to learn when to use it. You can't translate the German 'Perfekt' into the present perfect. It is very important that you learn when to use the present perfect in English. Let's have a look.

Achtung: Du kannst nicht immer im Englischen Present Perfect verwenden, wenn du im Deutschen das Perfekt verwendest. Also achte auf die Regeln!

1. We use the **present perfect** for actions that have happened in the **recent past** and have **result** on the **present situation**. We do not usually say when these actions took place.
   → Ereignisse, die kürzlich stattgefunden haben und eine Auswirkung bis in die Gegenwart haben!

   Examples

   The teacher **has closed** the window. → The window is closed now.
   She **has broken** her foot. → She can't run.
   I **have dropped** the bottle. → There is glass all over the floor.
   My parents **have gone** shopping. → They are not at home yet.

2. The **present perfect** is also used with time expressions for **unfinished time**. The action has taken place in the past but the 'time' isn't finished.
   - today
   - this week
   - this month
   - this year
   - this summer

   Examples

   Have you **seen** Peter **today**?
   Hast du Peter heute gesehen?
   The boys **haven't spoken** to their grandparents **this month**?
   Die Jungs haben diesen Monat (noch) nicht mit ihren Großeltern gesprochen.
   He **hasn't had** a cold once **this year**.
   In diesem Jahr hatte er noch keine Erkältung (gehabt).

3. We use the **present perfect** with the following **time adverbials.** Please look at the position of these words in the examples.
   - **just, only, just** (gerade, soeben)
   - **recently, lately** (kürzlich, vor kurzem, in letzter Zeit)
   - **so far** (bisher, bislang, bis jetzt)

   Examples

   My daughter **has just fed** the cat. (**just** →between have/has and main verb)
   I **haven't seen** Bella **recently**. (**recently/lately** → after the object)
   I **have answered** nine questions **so far**. (**so far** → after the object)

4. We also use the present perfect with **'already'** (schon, bereits) and **'yet'** (schon, noch nicht).

   'already' is normally used in **positive sentences**.

   'yet' is used in **negative sentences** and **questions**.

   Examples

   She has **already taken** a photo. ('**already**' → in front of the main verb)

   They **haven't organised** their holiday **yet**. ('**yet**' →after the object)

   Have you **finished** the test **yet**? ('**yet**' →after the object)

5. '**ever**' (in questions) and '**never**' can also be used with the **present perfect** to talk about actions that have or have not happened in our lives up to now.

   Examples

   Have you **ever** **seen** Queen Elizabeth? →Hast du jemals Queen Elisabeth gesehen?

   I **have** **never** **slept** in a water bed. → Ich habe noch nie in einem Wasserbett geschlafen

   Has Stuart **ever been*** to Scotland? → War Stuart je in Schottland (ist gewesen)?

   * 'been' (to be) can be used in the present perfect to say that we have gone somewhere and come back.

   Compare

   She **has been** to Barcelona. (She is back.)
   → Sie ist in Barcelona gewesen. / Sie war in Barcelona.

   She **has gone** to Barcelona. (She is still in Barcelona.)
   → Sie ist nach Barcelona gefahren. (und ist immer noch dort)

6. The present perfect is used to talk about an action that **started in the past and is continuing**. The emphasis (Gewichtung/Betonung) is not on the action itself but on '**how long**'. We use '**since**' or '**for**' to say how long. '**Since**' is used to describe a **'point of time'** and '**for**' is used to '**describe a period of time**'. → Sowohl 'since' als auch 'for' werden mit 'seit' übersetzt, wobei **since** verwendet wird, wenn man einen genauen Zeitpunkt angibt und '**for**' , wenn es sich um einen **Zeitraum** handelt.

   Examples

   I **have been** here **since eight o'clock**. → Ich bin hier seit 8:00 Uhr.

   We **have known** each other **for twenty five years**. → Wir kennen uns seit 25 Jahren.

   Julia **has lived** in Munich **since 1997**. → Julia lebt seit 1997 in München.

Exercise 12

Put the following phrases in the correct order to make sentences in the present perfect. Underline the keyword for the present perfect, please.

1. *your parents / Simon /never/ has / met*

____

____

2. *have/ the books /ordered / The Robinsons / already*

____

____

3. *you / chocolates/ have / so far / how many /eaten/?*

____

____

4. *just /we/ learned /the present perfect/have/ about*

____

____

5. *she / yet / has / invited / to the party / her best friend /?*

____

____

6. *today /has / had a break / he/ ?*

____

____

1.6 Present Perfect - Simple Past

1.6.1 Revision: Simple Past (Wiederholung)

You learned the simple past last year. Let's have a quick look at the simple past again so that we can remember what it is all about.

The simple past is used when we talk about actions or events that happened in the past.

Positive

The simple past is formed by adding 'ed' to the verb or using an irregular past form

Examples

We **played** football last weekend.

Mark's dad **took** him to school yesterday.

They **found** some money under the sofa.

I **lived** in England when I was young.

Negative

The simple past is formed in the negative using 'did not' or 'didn't'. (except with the verb 'to be')

Examples

We **weren't** at the park all day yesterday.

I **did not buy** any football magazines last month.

We **didn't need** our book two weeks ago.

The snake **didn't bite** the little boy.

Questions

Questions are formed with 'did'. (except the verb 'to be')

Examples

Was your son late for the bus?

Where **did you go** after school two days ago?

Did you talk to the teacher about the field trip?

What did you have for dinner yesterday evening?

Exercise 13

*Put the following sentences into the **simple past**.*

1. *I ____________________ (to go out) with my friends yesterday.*
2. *The swimming pool ______________________ (to be/not) open last weekend.*
3. *The dog _____________________ (to run) down the road and barked at the postman.*
4. *We _________________________ (to read/not) the whole book.*
5. *________ the little girl __________ (to get on/?) the bus?*
6. *Julius' pony ____________________ (to eat/not) all its food.*

1.6.2 Comparison: Present Perfect - Simple Past

You have to know when to use the simple past and when to use the present perfect. It is important that you do not translate but **'think English'**.

The table below shows the differences.

simple past	present perfect
finished time yesterday, last week, last month, in 1989, on Sunday, when I was young, this morning* etc. I drank a lot of water yesterday.	**unfinished time** today, this week, this month, this morning * etc. I have drunk a lot of water today.
key words yesterday, last…………, in ……….(year), ………….ago	**key words** just, recently, so far, already, yet, until now, (ever, never)**
action completed in the past – no direct result in the present (often with a finished time expression) I **went** to school in America. (*no direct result*) We **saw** a man with one leg when we were in New York. The students **took** the test 3 weeks ago.	**recent action – results in the present** I have told Jim about the homework. *Jim knows about the homework.* She has cleaned the car. *The car is clean*
finished action (how long/when) I **lived** in India for twenty years. *I don't live there now.* Sylvia **had** a dog when she was a child. *She doesn't have the dog anymore.*	**unfinished action (how long)** **for /since** I **have lived** in India for twenty years. (*I still live in India*) Sylvia **has had** a dog since May. *She still has the dog.*

* 'this morning' can be used with either the simple past or the present perfect. It depends what time it is when the speaker is speaking. Is 'the morning' finished or unfinished?

10.00am I have seen James this morning.
5.00pm I saw James this morning

** **ever and never** are **key words for the present perfect** because they imply unfinished time
→ **ever und never** werden **immer** mit dem **Present Perfect** verwendet, weil sie unbeendete Zeit implizieren.

Have Mike and Rose ever **been** to China? (their lives - unfinished)
She **has** never **eaten** Sushi. (her life - unfinished)

Exercise 14

Look at the dialogue and decide if the verbs are in the simple past or present perfect. Can you say why each tense is used?

James is visiting Catherine at her home in Virginia. It is 1.00 pm.

Catherine:	*Hello James. It is wonderful to see you.*
James:	*Hi Catherine. How are you? It is great to see you too.*
Catherine:	*How long did your journey take? What time did you leave this morning?*
James:	*I left at 8.00 am. It was a long journey. I travelled by train. Your house is very nice. How long have you lived here?*
Catherine:	*I have lived here since April. I haven't finished unpacking yet. There is still a lot to do but don't worry I have already unpacked the kitchen things. Would you like a cup of tea? You have been on a long journey.*
James:	*Oh yes please. I would love a cup of tea.*
Catherine:	*Are you hungry?*
James:	*No thanks. I have just eaten. I had a sandwich at the station.*
Catherine:	*OK then. Let's go into the kitchen.*

1.7 Future Tenses – 'will' and 'going to'

This year you are expected to learn two future tenses. The 'will' future (simple future) and the 'going to future'.

1.7.1 Going to Future

Last year you learned how to use the 'going to' future. Let's review. (→ Wiederholung vom letzten Jahr)

1.7.1.1 Form

The basic form is as follows:

Positive /negative sentences

subject	to be(not)+ going to	verb	object	place/ time
Our friends	are going to	visit	us	next summer.
He	isn't going to	work		next weekend.
I	am going to	study	for the test	this weekend.
We	aren't going to	miss	the bus.	

Yes / no questions are formed by switching the subject and the verb 'to be'.

to be	subject	going to	verb	object	place/time
Is	Sylvia	going to	make	the trifle?	
Are	Nina and Bella	going to	buy	some new shoes	in Munich?
Is	it	going to	rain?		

***Exercise* 15**

You can add **question words** for more specific information. Try to translate the sentences.

Who is going to answer the email?

____

How many teenagers are going to come to the party?

____

When is it going to stop raining?

____

Why is the trainer going to quit?

____

Whose father is going to pick up the children?

____

1.7.1.2 Function

1. We use the **going to future** when we want to talk about **plans or intentions**. These are plans and **not 100%** sure. (→ going to future wird verwendet bei Plänen, die **nicht sicher** sind)

Christine **is going to watch** TV all evening. → (Maybe a friend calls and she decides to go out / Vielleicht ruft ein Freund(in) an und sie entscheidet sich auszugehen)
I **am going to do** my homework straight after school. → (This is definitely a plan!)
We **aren't going to be** late. → (Hopefully not! We plan to be on time)
Andrew **is going to sleep in** (ausschlafen) tomorrow morning. → (Maybe the dog will wake him up!)

2. We also use the **going to future** when we talk about something we **expect** to happen. There is normally something that we can see, feel or hear that tells us that something is going to happen. This is a prediction (Prognose) **or** forecast with evidence (Vorhersage mit Beweis).

➔ Look! He **is going to fall off** the ladder. (The ladder is wobbly (wackelig).)
➔ It's late! You **are going to miss** the train. (It is late.)
➔ Oh no! The baby is going to cry. ( Look at his face!)

Exercise 16

Fill in the correct form of the going to future and say whether it is a plan ***or*** *a prediction (with evidence) (Vorhersage mit Beweis).*

1. *Emily __________________ (to learn) how to ride a bike next summer.*
plan/prediction

2. *The sun________________ (to shine).*
plan/prediction

3. *She _____________(to have) a baby. (In English 'to have a baby' means ein Baby bekommen')*

plan/prediction

4. *My mum ________________(to bake) a cake this afternoon.*
plan/prediction

1.7.2 Future Simple – Will Future

The 'will future' or 'future simple' is a complex tense which can be used in many different situations. We have presented two main uses of the 'will future' but these uses are not the only times when we use 'will'.

➔ Das 'will'-Future ist eine komplexe Zeitform. Wir stellen hier zwei Einsatzmöglichkeiten vor, dies sind aber bei weitem nicht alle.

1.7.2.1 Form

The **will future** is formed using **will + bare infinitive.**

subject	will (not)	verb	object/place /time
It	won't (will not)	rain	next week.
I	will	make	you a sandwich.
Our teacher	won't (will not)	give	us a test next week.
The secretary	will	call	your mum for you.

In spoken English we usually use the short form. The **short form** is formed by adding **'ll** to the **subject**.

I'll, you'll, he'll, she'll, it'll, we'll, they'll

The **negative short form** is '**won't**'.

A question is formed by switching the subject and will.

He **will** be late. → **Will** he be late?

It **will** take six hours to get there. → How long **will** it take to get there?

Short answers to yes or no questions are formed (as usual – wie immer) using the first word of the question.

question	yes answer	no answer
Will it snow at Christmas?	Yes, it **will**.	No, it **won't**.
Will the dog chase us?	Yes, it **will**.	No, it **won't**.
Will all the children pass the test?	Yes, they **will**.	No, they **won't**.

1.7.2.2 Function

1. We use **'will'** when we want to talk about **predictions or forecasts**, but **without evidence**. We use **'will'** when we want to give an opinion or speculate about the future. These are usually events that we cannot influence.
   ➔ Das 'will-future' wird verwendet, wenn man über zukünftige Ereignisse spricht ohne ein festes Anzeichen dafür (z.B. Wettervorhersage)
   ➔ Wenn wir Vermutungen oder Spekulationen über die Zukunft von uns geben
   → Häufig verwenden wir im gesprochenen Deutsch nur Präsens und kein Futur

The sun will shine on my birthday.	→ An meinem Geburtstag wird die Sonne scheinen.
I think **John will become** class representative.	→ Ich glaube John wird heute Klassensprecher werden.
I am sure **the teacher will be** on time.	→Ich bin sicher der Lehrer kommt pünktlich.
Perhaps **the price will go up**.	→Vielleicht steigen die Preise an. (werden ansteigen).

In all these examples we have no way of knowing if these events will really take place, which is why we use 'will'. They are only **predictions**. (→ alles nur Vorhersagen/Prognosen **<u>ohne</u> Garantie**)

We often use the following **expressions with 'will'**.

I'm sure, I think, I don't think, I expect, I hope, I suppose, I believe, I'm afraid, I wonder if, surely, perhaps, probably**

* we don't say

I think he **won't** be late. (**falsch**) – Ich glaube, er wird nicht zu spät kommen

BUT

I don't think he **will** be late. – Ich glaube nicht, dass er zu spät kommt

➔ Auch im Deutschen ist die zweite Variante die bessere!

Merke:	**The negative is on the 'think' part of the sentence not the 'will' part.**

** <u>probably</u> (wahrscheinlich) does not go at the front of the sentence but <u>between the subject and verb</u>.
(probably steht zwischen Subjekt und Prädikat bzw. nach dem Hilfsverb)

➔ He will **probably** answer all the questions correctly.

2. **'Will'** is also used when we make decisions at the time of speaking. **'Will'** is **not used** for actions that we have planned. These decisions are called **spontaneous decisions (spontane Entscheidung)**.

   \`will-future' verwenden wir, wenn wir etwas spontan entscheiden (z.B. spontane Hilfe anbieten)

   John says, 'I'm thirsty'- you say, **'I'll get you a drink'**.
   ➔ You decided to get John a drink when he said that he was thirsty. (spontaneously)

   The phone rings. You say **'I'll answer it'**.
   ➔ You decided to answer the phone when you heard it ringing.

   You teacher says, **'Who will give Anna the homework**?' Jack says, 'I **will**'.
   ➔ Jack decided to give Anna the homework <u>spontaneously</u> →when the teacher asked.

Exercise 17

Fill in the spaces with the correct form of 'will'. Decide if the sentence/question is a prediction or a spontaneous decision, underline the correct answer.

1. *Angela Merkel ________ probably ___________ the election (die Wahl).*

   prediction/spontaneous decision

2. *'I have lost my key'. 'I __________ help you look for it.'*

   prediction/spontaneous decision

3. *The fortune teller (die Wahrsagerin) said that I __________ (not) get married.*

   prediction/spontaneous decision

4. *Don't worry, it ___________ (not) rain there isn't a cloud in the sky.*

   prediction/spontaneous decision

5. *'I can't carry all these books. ___________ you help me please?'*

   prediction /spontaneous decision

6. *I don't think we ____________have a test tomorrow.*

   prediction /spontaneous decision

1.7.3 Comparison – Going to – Will

In your tests you will have to decide when to use the 'will future' (future simple) and when to use the 'going to' future.

going to	will
predictions <u>with</u> evidence	**predictions <u>without</u> evidence**
(boy on diving board) He **is going to jump** into the water. Look at the angry bear! He **is going to kill** the hunter!	I think it **will snow** tomorrow. Our biology teacher **won't give** us a quiz.
plans	**spontaneous decisions**
Next weekend we **are going to go** shopping.	'I'm thirsty.' – **'I'll** get you some water.'

Exercise 18

Choose the correct tense to complete the sentences/questions. Cross out the incorrect tense.

1. *In 100 years everybody* ***is going to/will*** *travel to the moon.*
2. *Mary has hurt her leg. I* ***am going to / will*** *call a doctor.*

3. *Look at that man. He* ***is going to/will*** *drop the pizza!*
4. *I hope he* ***is going to /will*** *call me later.*
5. *What do you think you* ***are going to/ will*** *get for Christmas?*
6. *The Smiths* ***are going to/will*** *go on holiday with their friends next year.*

1.8 Conditional Clauses (If - sentences)

This year you have to learn conditional sentences (type 0 and type 1) in English. Conditional sentences are not difficult; you just have to learn the rules.

Konditionalsätze sind nicht schwer, wenn du dich an ein paar Regeln hältst.

A conditional sentence has two clauses (parts), the **'if' clause** and the '**main clause**'.

1.8.1 Conditional Clauses -Type 0

Type 0 conditional sentences are used to talk about situations that are **always true like facts** (Fakten).

Examples

- If the temperature of water reaches 100°C, it boils.
- If you press the button, the machine goes off.

Type 0 conditional sentences are formed using the **simple present in both the main clause** and **the 'if' clause**.

1.8.2 Conditional Clauses - Type 1

Type 1 'if'-sentences are used when the **situation is real and possible**. The 'if'-part of the sentence is usually probable (Der 'if-part' ist möglich).

Examples

- If the teacher gives us a test, I will get a good mark.
- We will go home if it rains.
- If I see Rory, I can tell him about the party.
- If the teacher asks, tell him about the missing homework.

Form

It is important to know how to form conditional sentences. The 'if' part of the sentence is the 'condition' (something that will probably happen). The main clause is the consequence of this condition.

➔ Der Konditionalsatz - if-Clause - ist die Bedingung, die möglicherweise eintrifft, der Hauptsatz ist die Konsequenz daraus.

Conditional Clauses

If-sentences

if clause	main clause
If it **snows,**	the children **will wear** boots **(will)**
If it **doesn't rain,**	we **will have** a picnic. **(will)**
If the dogs **don't bark,**	no one **will know** we are here. **(will)**
If you **are** late,	the teacher **won't be** happy. **(will)**
If you **see** a mouse,	**don't feed** it , please. **(imperative)**
If they **don't arrive,**	**call** the police! **(imperative)**
If you **do** your homework,	you **can go** out. **(modal verb)**
If Robert **doesn't pass** his exams,	he **can't go** university. **(modal verb)**
If we **go** to California,	we **may see** a film star. **(modal verb)**

Rules

1. The **'if' clause** is formed using the **simple present.** Don't forget that the simple present is formed using 'doesn't' or 'don't' in the negative.

2. **Don't** put '**will**' in the '**if clause**'.

*'**if** and **will** makes me **ill**'*

3. You can put the **'if' clause or the main clause** first. It doesn't matter, **BUT** you must make sure you have a **comma** if the **'if' clause is at the beginning**.
   Nur wenn der if-Satz vorne steht, muss der Hauptsatz durch ein Komma abgetrennt werden!
   - If Rebecca cleans the living room**,** I will clean the kitchen. (comma)
   - I will clean the kitchen if Rebecca cleans the living room. (**no** comma)

4. The **main clause** is usually formed using the **'will' future.**
   ➔ The 'will' future is **will + verb** (bare infinitive) or will not (won't) + verb.
   ➔ It is also possible to use the **imperative** in the **main clause**.
   The imperative is formed using the main verb (bare infinitive) or don't + infinitive

   You can **replace 'will'** with the modal verb **'can', 'cannot' (can't), 'may' or 'may not'.**
   Modal verbs are followed by the bare infinitive,; there is more information in 1.9.
   Anstatt 'will' kannst du auch eines der Hilfsverben (can, may, + Verneinung) verwenden gefolgt von dem ‚bare infinitive'

The '**bare infinitive**' is the infinitive without 'to'.

Exercise 19: *Put the verbs in the **correct form** to make conditional sentences and put in the **comma where necessary**. (richtiges Verb und Komma, wenn nötig!)*

1. *If Lena ____________ (to buy) that expensive dress she won't have any money left (=übrig).*
2. *We can't get home if we _____________ (not/find) a taxi.*
3. *If our team wins the cup we_________________ (to celebrate).*
4. *If you don't feel better ______________ (to go/imperative) to the doctor.*
5. *I can tell them if I ______________(to see)them.*
6. *_______________(not/ tell/ imperative) him if he doesn't ask.*

1.8.3 If – when – falls/wenn

'If' can be translated as **'falls'** or **'wenn'** in conditional sentences.

If the sun shines, we will go to the beach.

→**Wenn** die Sonne scheint gehen wir zum Strand. **oder**

→**Falls** die Sonne scheint, gehen wir zum Strand.

In all of the examples above we do not know if the sun will shine or not. It is a condition that is probable (Es ist eine Bedingung die wahrscheinlich ist) We will **only** go to the beach if the sun shines.

'When' has a different meaning to **'if'**. Please look at the examples below.
Das englische 'when' wird ebenso mit 'wenn' im Deutschen übersetzt, es gelten dieselben Regeln wie im 'if-clause', aber es hat eine andere Bedeutung.

When the lesson finishes, we will go home.
→ Wenn die Stunde zu Ende ist, gehen wir nach Hause.

We are **sure** the lesson will finish and then we will go home.

If Nick calls, I will tell him about the test.
→ Wenn (falls) Nick anruft, erzähle ich ihm von der Probe.

I am **not sure** if Nick will phone or not. I will tell him about the test **only** if he calls. (→ nur falls er anruft, es ist nicht sicher, dass er anruft)

→ 'If' wird verwendet für Möglichkeiten, wir wissen nicht ob sie eintreten. 'when' wird verwendet bei Ereignissen, die sicher eintreten.

Exercise 20

Fill in the spaces with either 'if' or 'when'.

1. *____________Susie is 18, she will get her driving license.*
2. *____________ you are not at school tomorrow, I will photocopy the homework.*
3. *Rebecca reads ____________she goes to bed.*
4. *______________you don't study, you won't pass the test.*
5. *_______________ you get home, tell your mum about the parent teacher conference.*
6. *You can go to the cinema ____________ you get a good mark on the test.*

1.9 Modal Verbs

Last year you learned how to use the modal verbs 'can', 'must' and 'needn't'.

This year you will learn 'when' to use these verbs and the past and future tenses of these verbs.

Peter **can`t go** out tonight.

I **can swim**.

Children **must do** their homework.

You **mustn't smoke**.

German school children **needn't go** to school at weekends.

The bare infinitive is the infinitive without 'to'

Remember: a **modal verb** is always followed by the main verb in the bare infinitive.

Look at these sentences and see what function the modal verb has.

1. He **can dance**.
2. You **can't go** to the cinema. You **mustn't eat** too many sweets.
3. You **must study** for your exams.
4. The children **needn't do** any homework in the holidays. ☺

Exercise 21

Translate the sentences above.

1. ____

2. ____

3. ____

4. ____

You can see that '**can**' has two functions. It can be used to give somebody (or something) **permission** (Erlaubnis) to do something or it can be used to say that somebody (or something) has the **ability (**Fähigkeit**)** to do something.

You **can go** to the party.	→ **permission (**Erlaubnis**)**
A kangaroo **can jump** very high.	→ **ability (**Fähigkeit**)**

'**Must**' and '**needn't**' are both used to express **obligation** and/or **necessity**.

A child **must go** to school.	→ **obligation (**Pflicht**)**
You **needn't wear** a jacket in the summer.	→ **necessity (**Notwendigkeit**)**

1.9.1 Modal Verbs – ability - can

We use the modal verb **'can'** to express **ability**. The infinitive of **'can'** is **'to be able to'**. Let's look at some examples in the **past, present and future**.

Present 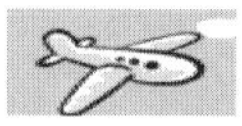

Pilots **can fly** aeroplanes.
Dogs **cannot (can't)** fly aeroplanes.
Pilots **are able to fly** aeroplanes.
Dogs **aren't able to fly** aeroplanes.

can
am/is/are,
able to

Past 

Simon **could swim** when he was two.
Christopher and James **couldn't (could not) swim** when they were two.
Simon **was able to swim** when he was two.
Christopher and James **weren't able to swim** when they were two.

could
was/were
able to

Future 

You **will be able to drive** when you are eighteen.
Baby Jim **won't be able to drive** next week.
It is also possible to use 'can' for the future.
Can you help me with my new computer next week?
My dad **can repair** your car for you tomorrow.

will/won't be able to

can/can´t

Exercise 22

Fill in the gaps with the correct form of 'can'. Remember there are sometimes two possible answers.

1. *How many languages ____________________ speak?*
2. *My right hand is broken. I ____________________________ take the test tomorrow.*
3. *Mary has lost her mobile phone. She ______________________________ send any text messages yesterday.*
4. *_______ the school _____________________ organise an exchange programme with a French school next year?*
5. *Richard ______________________ play football but he __________________ (not) play tennis.*
6. *The children didn't pass the test because they _____________________ remember many of the words.*

1.9.2 Modal Verbs – Permission- can- may- mustn't

We use the modal verbs '**can**' and '**may**' to ask for and give **permission**. 'May' is more formal than can. The **infinitive** of '**can/may**' is '**to be allowed to'**. We use '**must not**' when we want to say that something is **forbidden**.

*'Mum, **can** my friends sleep over tonight?'*

'Mum, **may** I sleep over at Rory's house tonight?'
The infinitive of **'can'** or **'may'** is **'to be allowed to'**.

can
may
am/is/are allowed to
mustn´t

Present

May I watch the late film tonight? Yes, you **may.**

Can I watch TV?

(It is unusual to use 'to be allowed to' for a **request**. We usually use '**may I**' or '**can I'**.)

Bob, you **are allowed to stay up** until midnight.

My son **isn't allowed to go** watch horror films.

You **mustn't smoke** at petrol stations .

was/were allowed to

Past 

Rebecca **was allowed to** play outside in the summer.

The children **weren't allowed to jump** around in the bus when they went to Munich.

We **weren't allowed to leave** the classroom before the teacher.

Important

We **cannot** use **'could'** as the past of 'can' when we are talking about giving **permission** for something specific.

Future

In five years **you will be allowed to get** your driving licence.

In 100 years teenagers **will be allowed to fly** aeroplanes.

You **won't be allowed to buy** a children's ticket on the bus next year.

Exercise 23

Fill in the correct form of can/may.

1. *______________________ I borrow your book?*
2. *You must go to bed early tonight. You ____________________ stay out late last night.*
3. *Dogs ____ (not) go into the children's play area.*
4. *The children _________________________ (not) copy their friends' homework.*
5. *You ___________________________________ go to the city alone when you are fifteen.*
6. *Mary _______________________________ (not) sleep at her friend's house last night.*

1.9.3 Modal Verbs – Obligation and Necessity -have to –need -must

We use the '**must**', '**have to**' and '**need**' to express obligation and necessity (Pflicht und Notwendigkeit).

The difference between 'must' and 'have to'

A lot of German people use 'must' a lot when they are speaking English because it sounds like the German 'müssen'. In English we use 'must' when the obligation comes from the speaker.

- You **must clean** your room before you go out.
  Your mum says this because she wants you to clean your room.
- You **must take** your shoes **off** before you come into the living room.
  The speaker wants you to do this.
- You **have to work** hard before the test.
  This is necessary so that you pass the test.
- You **have to be** careful when you cross the road.
  It is necessary to be careful so that you don't get hit by a car.

Let's have a look at '**have to**'.

Positive

'**have to**' means that there is **an obligation or necessity** to do something.

subject	have to/has to	verb	object /place/time
I	**have to**	catch	the bus at 6.45am
you	**have to**	finish	your breakfast.
we	**have to**	clean	the kitchen.
they	**have to**	help	their little brother.
he	**has to**	get up	early.
she	**has to**	go	to the bakery.
it	**has to**	sleep	in the garden .

have to

has to

Negative

'**have to**' in the **negative** means that there is **no obligation or necessity** to do something.
'**don't have to**' or '**doesn't have to**' have the same meaning as '**needn't**'.

He **doesn't have to go** to the dentist.

He **needn't go** to the dentist.

subject	don't /doesn't have to	verb	object /place/time
I	**don't have to**	go	to school at weekends.
you	**don't have to**	get up	early in the holidays.
we	**don't have to**	take	the bus.
they	**don't have to**	work	on Sundays.
he	**doesn't have to**	eat	all the vegetables.
she	**doesn't have to**	help	her dad in the garden.
it	**doesn't have to**	work!	

don't have to
doesn´t have to
needn't

Question

do/does	subject	have to	verb	object /place/time
Do	you	**have to**	read	the whole book?
	we	**have to**	wear	school uniform?
	they	**have to**	sit	at the front of the class?
Does	he	**have to**	wear	a coat in winter?
	she	**have to**	answer	all the questions?
	it	**have to**	sleep	in the dog house?

do you have to
does he have to

Exercise 24

Fill in the gaps with the correct form of 'have to'.

1. *Sylvia ____________________ take the train to London because her car is broken.*
2. *__________ Anna ____________ wear glasses?*
3. *Andrew __________________ take his dog to the vet. He has hurt his foot.*
4. *Louise ______________________ help the children with their homework. They can do it themselves.*
5. *The students __________________ learn their vocabulary.*
6. *______________ you ________________ write an essay in English this year?*

Past

The **past** of 'have to' is '**had to**'.

There is **<u>no past</u> of 'must'** so we use **<u>'had to</u>'**.

had to
didn't have to

- We **had to wear** hats this morning because it was snowing.
- John **had to pay** for the book himself. He had damaged it.
- I **had to phone** the doctor because I felt ill.

- He **didn't have to go** to school because he had a cold.
- We **didn't have to answer** all the questions on the test. We were allowed to choose three.
- The children **didn't have to** get up early this morning because it is Sunday.

Future

It is normal to use the present form of modal verbs in future sentences.
Es ist üblich die Gegenwartsform mit einem Hilfsverb zu verwenden statt Futur.

- **I have to work** tomorrow.
- She **doesn't have to go** to the dentist until next year.
- You **must come** home on time tonight.

will have to
won't have to

There is, however, a future form.

The **future simple** is formed with '**will + have to'.**

- Bill **will have to pay** for the meal next week. It is his turn.
- I hope we **won't have to wait** too long for the bus.
- There is some bread in the cupboard. We **won't have to buy** any this afternoon.
  Es ist etwas Brot im Schrank. Wir **werden** kein Brot **kaufen müssen** (wörtlich)

Exercise 25

Fill in the correct form of 'have to'.

1. *We ___________________ change planes in London. It was a direct flight.*
2. *Last night Mary _______________________ borrow some money from her friends because she had forgotten her purse.*
3. *I think he _________________ take the test when he comes back to school.*
4. *'Hey, you have just broken my pen. You _______________ buy me a new one.'*

6. *Christopher stayed late after school because he _____________ speak to the teacher about the homework.*

7. *Last Friday Mike __________________ help his mum in the kitchen. It was his birthday.*

1.9.4 Summary Modal Verbs

	ability Fähigkeit	permission Erlaubnis	obligation and necessity Pflicht/Notwendigkeit
present	can/can't am/is/are(not) able to	can may am/is /are (not) allowed to mustn't	must have to /don't have to has to/ doesn't have to needn't
past	could/couldn't was/were able to	was/were(not) allowed to	had to /didn't have to
future	will/won't be able to	will/won't be allowed to	will have to

Exercise 26

Fill in the correct modal verb in the correct tense. There may be more than one possible answer.

1. *Ronald ____________________________ (not) swim today because he has broken his arm.*
2. *I am so late. I ________________________ hurry.*
3. *If you don't pass your driving test you ____________________________ (not) drive.*
4. *________________________ I borrow your calculator, please?*
5. *You ____________________________ eat all the ice cream. I want some.*
6. *Bella did her homework yesterday. She ______________________ (not) do her homework today.*

1.10 Defining Relative Clauses

1.10.1 What is a defining relative clause?

A clause contains a subject and a verb. You can have an **independent clause** (Hauptsatz) - which can stand alone or a **dependent clause** (Nebensatz) - which cannot stand alone. (also called a subordinate clause)

→Ein Satz besteht aus mindestens einem Subjekt und einem Prädikat (Bsp.: Nina schläft). Wir unterscheiden Haupt- und Nebensätze. Nur ein Hauptsatz kann alleine stehen.

A **defining relative clause** (Relativsatz) is used to give us **more information** so that we know 'who' or 'what' we are talking about. A **defining relative clause cannot stand alone**. It is a **dependent clause**.

→Ein Relativsatz ist ein Nebensatz und kann nicht alleine stehen, er gibt uns nähere Informationen zum Hauptsatz.

Examples

The lady **who came to our house** was friendly.

→ Die Dame, die zu uns nach Hause kam, war freundlich.

We can break this sentence down into two clauses. (→ Aufteilung in 2 Satzteile)

The lady was friendly. (**independent clause**/ (Unabhängiger) Hauptsatz)

who came to our house (defining relative clause (dependent clause) / Relativsatz**)**

The 'who came to our house' clause tells us 'which' lady we are talking about. It '**identifies or defines**' the lady.

The dog **which barks all night** lives next door to us.
→ Der Hund, der die ganze Nacht bellte, lebt im Nachbarhouse.
The dog lives next door to us. (independent clause/ Hauptsatz)

which barks all night (defining relative clause (dependent clause) / Relativsatz)

Again we know here which dog we are talking about because we say which dog→ the dog which barks all night.

Position

A defining relative clause goes as close to the person or thing we are talking about as possible.
→ Der Relativsatz kommt direkt nach der Person oder Sache, auf die er sich bezieht.

Commas

There are **no commas in defining relative clauses**. → **kein Komma**

Achtung: Im Deutschen wird der Relativsatz immer durch ein Komma getrennt!

1.10.2 Relative pronouns in defining relative clauses.

Relative pronouns (Relativpronomen) are used in defining relative clauses.

Relative pronouns include:

which, whose, who or *whom, that, when, where, why*

... and are used as follows:

Person	**who, that, (whom), whose**
Thing	**which, that, whose,**
Place	**where**
Time	**when**

Examples

The mobile phone **which/that is on sale** is on the top shelf.

Das Handy, **welches/das im Angebot ist**, liegt im obersten Regal,

The lady **who/that takes my dog for a walk** is very nice.

Die Dame, **welche/die meinen Hund ausführte**, ist sehr nett.

The park **where the children play** is next to an ice cream shop.

Der Park, **in dem (wo) die Kinder spielen**, ist in der Nähe eines Eiscafés.

The picture **whose owner is unknown** was sold for £1

Das Bild, dessen Besitzer unbekannt ist, wurde für 1 £ verkauft.

The neighbour **whose son is in our class** is going to drive us to school.

Der Nachbar, **dessen Sohn in unsere Klasse geht**, wird uns in die Schule fahren.

I will never forget the Christmas **when he bought me a diamond ring.**

Ich werde nie das Weihnachtsfest vergessen, an dem er mir einen Diamantring kaufte.

1.10.3 Relative Pronouns replacing the subject of a sentence

A relative pronoun can replace the subject of a sentence.
Remember you use '**who**' for people, '**which**' for things and '**that**' for both people and things. As a general rule '**that**' is used in **spoken English** and not in formal texts.

Merke: „That" kann sowohl für Menschen als auch Dinge benutzt werden, findet den Einsatz jedoch hauptsächlich im Gesprochenen. In Texten bitte who und which verwenden.

Examples

The girls are pretty.

They are in my class.

↓

subject

↓

The girls **who/that** are in my class are pretty.

Don't eat meat.

It is not fresh.

↓

subject →

Don't eat meat **which/that** is not fresh.

Exercise 27

Put the two sentences/questions together. The subject is underlined.

1. *The boy is on our football team. <u>He</u> has got a broken leg.*

____

____

2. *Fizzy drinks aren't good for you. <u>They</u> have got a lot of sugar.*

____

____

3. *Have you seen the teacher? <u>He</u> comes from America.*

____

____

4. *The computer is broken. <u>It</u> is in the classroom.*

____

____

5. *The girl is unhappy. <u>She</u> lost the tennis match.*

____

____

6. *Do you know the man? <u>He</u> lives opposite us.*

____

____

1.10.4 Relative pronouns replacing the object of a sentence

A relative pronoun can also replace the object of a sentence.

Remember you use ‘**who(m)**’ for people, ‘**which**’ for things and ‘**that**’ for both people and things. As a general rule ‘**that**’ is used in **spoken English** and not in formal texts.

‘Whom’ is **formal**. We usually use ‘who’ instead of ‘whom’.

When you replace the **object** of a sentence it is also **possible to leave out the relative pronoun (Ø).**

Relativpronomen können auch ein Objekt ersetzen. „Who/whom“ wird bei Personen verwendet, „which“ bei Sachen/Dingen und im gesprochenen Englisch kann man “that” für beides verwenden. Wenn man das Objekt ersetzt, kann das Relativpronomen auch weggelassen werden (Ø → kein Pronomen).

The lady has got green hair.

I saw **her (the lady)**.

↓

object

↓

The lady **who/that/Ø** I saw has got green hair.

The CD is fantastic.

I bought **it (the CD)** yesterday.

↓

object

↓

The CD **which/that/Ø** I bought yesterday is fantastic.

A good trick to help you decide if you can leave out (weglassen) **the relative pronoun is to see if there is a subject in the defining relative clause.**

In den obigen Beispielen kannst du jeweils auch das Relativpronomen weglassen. Dies kannst du in der Regel (i.d.R.) immer machen, wenn der Relativsatz ein eigenes Subjekt hat.

You are learning a language which/that/Ø **you** can speak all over the world.

↓

Subject (so it’s possible to leave the pronoun out)

➔ You are learning a language you can use all over the world.

Exercise 28

Put the two sentences/questions together. The object is underlined.

1. *I liked the girls. We met them at summer camp.*

2. *Mr Jones found the key. Emily was looking for it.*

3. *Where is the milk? I bought it yesterday.*

4. *Sylvia sent me the pictures. I wanted them.*

5. *Did you see the doctor? I like him?*

6. *Where is the telephone number? I wrote it down yesterday.*

1.10.5 Using the relative pronoun 'whose'.

'whose' can be used for both **people and things** in defining relative clauses.

Examples

I saw the boy. **His father** works with my dad.

I saw the boy **whose father** works for my dad.

➔ Ich besuchte den Jungen, dessen Vater für meinen Vater arbeitet.

There is a snake in the zoo. **Its teeth** are really dangerous.

There is a snake in the zoo **whose teeth** are really dangerous.

➔ Es gibt eine Schlange im Zoo, deren Zähne sehr gefährlich sind.

Exercise 29

Put the sentences/question together using 'whose'.

1. *I live in a city. Its history goes back many years.*

____

____

2. *The girl didn't get a good mark on the test. Her mother is talking to the teacher*

____

____

3. *John passed the test. His father is a professor.*

____

____

4. *The house is not for sale. Its value is unknown.*

____

____

1.10.6 Using the relative pronouns 'when' and 'where' .
We use the relative pronoun '**when**' for **time** and '**where**' for **places**

Examples

Hollywood is a place **where** film stars live.

Next year we are going to go on holiday to a country **where** the sun always shines.

Thursday 28th November was the day **when** we won the match.

December is the month **when** we celebrate Christmas.

Note: we often leave out 'when' in defining relative clauses.

1.10.7 Non - defining relative clauses (contact clauses)
A **non-defining relative clause** is different to a defining relative clause.
Ein unbestimmter Relativsatz ist für den Sinn des Satzes nicht notwendig, sondern gibt zusätzliche Informationen.

1. A non-defining relative clause is **not essential** (entscheidend) to the meaning of the sentence.
   Catherine, who passed all her exams, is coming to visit us.
   The information that Catherine passed her exams is extra information (Zusatzinformation). We know who Catherine is.
2. We use **commas in non - defining** relative clauses.
   Brighton**, which suffers from great storms,** is a historical city.
3. We **do not use** the relative pronoun **'that'** in non-defining relative clauses.
   The boy **who/that lives next door to us** smokes. (defining relative clause)
   John Smith, **who/~~that~~** lives next door to us, smokes. (non-defining relative clause)
4. You cannot leave out the pronouns in non-defining relative clauses.
   John Smith, who I like, is in my class.
   It is not possible to say:
   John Smith, Ø I like, is in my class.

Exercise 30
Cross out the options you cannot use in the sentences.

1. *Chinese food,* ***who/which/that/Ø*** *I love, is available in all areas of the city.*
2. *Food* ***who/which/that/Ø*** *you cook at home always tastes better.*
3. *Teachers* ***who/which/that/Ø*** *don't give much homework are very popular with the children.*
4. *The jeans* ***who/which/that/Ø*** *we saw in the new shop were very expensive.*
5. *Manchester United,* ***who/which/that/Ø*** *is one of two teams in Manchester, is very successful.*
6. *Rebecca's father,* ***who/which/that/Ø*** *comes from Iran, helps her with her homework.*

1.10.8 Prepositions in relative clauses

There are some verbs which need prepositions in a sentence. Here are some examples.

to go to, to listen to, to work with, to stay at, to speak to, to live in, to come from, to live with, to talk about, to sit opposite, to jump on..........etc.

- ➔ My grandfather often **talks about** his school days.
- ➔ We **went to** Spain last year.

The position of the preposition in a relative clause depends whether the sentence is formal or informal.

formal sentence → preposition goes in front of the relative pronoun.

informal sentence → preposition goes at the end of the relative clause.

Compare

The man **to whom*** I spoke told us that the restaurant is open every day. →formal (defining) → *('whom' is formal for 'who' in relative clauses.)

The man (who, that, Ø) I **spoke to** told us that the restaurant is open every day. →informal (defining)

New York City, **about which the guide spoke**, is an exciting city. →formal (non - defining)

New York City, **which the guide spoke about**, is an exciting city. →informal (non- defining)

Here are some **more examples** of informal sentences with relative clauses using verbs with prepositions.

The school **which (that, Ø) I went to** closed down last year.

I love the film **which (that, Ø) you told me about**.

Mrs Standing, **who I work with**, lives in London.

Exercise 31

Put the two sentences together. (informal)

1. *I live in a town. The town has got two open air swimming pools.*
   The town ____
2. *Zoe stayed with a family. They have got an enormous dog.*
   The family ____
3. *We go to a doctor. He is a specialist.*
   The doctor ____
4. *I talk to a girl on the bus. She comes from Mexico.*
   The girl ____

Make the following informal sentences formal.

1. *The man I spoke to at the airport was from Brazil.*

____

2. *The old bed which the dog sleeps on is very comfortable.*

____

1.11 Some/Any/Every/No

1.11.1 Somebody - Someone-Something- Somewhere

Last year you learned that we use 'some' for **positive sentences** and in **requests** and **offers**.

- I have got **some** money in my pocket.
- Our teacher gave us **some** sweets yesterday.
- May I have **some** of that delicious cake, please?
- Would you like **some** tea?

We follow the **same rules** when we make word compounds with 'some' (zusammengesetzte Wörter mit some).

- There is **somebody (someone)*** in the classroom.
- Would you like **something** to eat?
- Next winter I would like to go **somewhere** warm.

someone = somebody

* 'someone' and 'somebody' (irgendeiner/irgendjemand) are synonyms.

In addition we use **somebody**, **something** or **somewhere** in questions when we **expect the answer to be positive** (... wenn wir erwarten, dass die Antwort positive ausfällt**).**

- Your friend is crying. You ask, 'Has **someone** hurt you?' because you think someone has hurt him/her.
- You come home and there is a lovely smell coming from the kitchen. You ask, 'Is there **something** in the oven?'

1.11.2 Anyone-anybody-anything-anywhere

Last year you learned that we use '**any**' in **questions** and **negative** sentences.

- Have you got **any** sweets?
- Is there **any** water in the jug?
- Christopher didn't buy **any** milk because there is some in the fridge.
- They haven't seen **any** of their friends for weeks.

We can also make word **compounds** using 'any' and follow the **same rules**.

- Did you go **anywhere** nice last weekend?
- Was there **anybody/anyone*** I know at the party?
- I can't eat **anything** sweet. I am on a diet.

anyone = anybody

*'anyone' and 'anybody are synonyms.

In addition **anybody**, **anything** or **anywhere** can be used in positive sentences when we want to say that **who, which or where is not important**.

➔ **anybody, anything oder anywhere** können auch in positiven Sätzen verwendet werden, wenn das wer, was oder wo keine Bedeutung hat.

- You can eat **anything** you like.
- It doesn't matter. Buy the bread **anywhere** you like.
- **Anyone** can join the baseball team. You don't have to be good.

Exercise 32

Fill in the spaces with somebody, something somewhere or anybody, anything or anywhere.

1. *There isn't ________________ good on the TV at the moment.*
2. *I can smell ________________ burning. Did you turn the oven off?*
3. *Jenny's mother is very strict. She isn't allowed to go ________________ after 6.00pm.*
4. *________________ is allowed to play in the park. There are no rules.*
5. *Andrew lives ________________ near the station.*
6. *Can ________________ help me please?*

1.11.3 No/No one /Nobody/Nothing/ Nowhere

The word 'no' can be used to make a positive sentence negative.

- There is **no** snow in Africa.
- Sally has **no** idea where the book is.
- I have **no** problem with the other students.
- **No** problem! (kein Problem!)

We can also use 'no' to make the word compounds.

- There is **nothing** to eat in the cupboard.
- The money was **nowhere** to be found.
- **No one (nobody)** visited me when I was in hospital.

no one = nobody

***No one** and **nobody** are synonyms..

We use '**no**' and **'no' word compounds** to replace '**not any**'.

- I have**n't** got **any** time to help you.
- I have **no** time to help you.

- We ca**n't** see **anything** in the dark.
- We can see **nothing** in the dark.

- Philip has**n't** been **anywhere** today.
- Philip has been **nowhere** today.

- I did**n't** see **anybody.**
- I saw **nobody.**

We also use **nobody (no one) or nothing** as the **subject** of a sentence.

- **No one** studied for the test.
- **Nothing** helped my cold. I am still ill.

Exercise 33

Fill in the spaces with no, nobody, nothing or nowhere.

1. *There is ____________________ in the fridge.*
2. *I have ______________ water left. I am really thirsty.*
3. *__________________________ is allowed to smoke in the playground.*
4. *We are bored. We have ___________________ to go and ________________ to do.*
5. *_______________________ phoned me on my birthday.*

1.11.4 Every/everybody / everyone/ everything/ everywhere

'**Every'** is used to mean '**all'**. We usually use '**every'** when we are talking about **a group**. It is used with **singular countable nouns**.

- I ate **every** apple in the bowl.
- **Every** student must take the test.
- The headmaster visited **every** class in the school.
- **Every** child in Germany has to go to school.

'every' is followed by singular countable nouns

We can also use 'every' to make word compounds.

- **Everybody/everyone** has to wear trainers in the gym.
- Louise listened to **everything** the teacher said.
- I have looked **everywhere** but I can't find my jacket.

Exercise 34

I. Fill in the spaces with every, everybody, everything or everywhere.

1. *___________________ likes our football trainer. He is very nice.*
2. *The teacher told us to answer ______________________ question on the test.*
3. *I was so hungry. I ate _______________________ I could find.*
4. *My boyfriend never walks. He goes __________________ by car.*

II. There is something wrong in the following sentences. Can you find the mistake?

1. *The boys drank every water in the bottle.*

____

2. *I can do every exercises in the book.*

____

2 Schulaufgaben/Klassenarbeiten

2.1 Short Test1 – Unit 1

Written English Short Test 1			**Unit 1**
October	**Your score _________**	**Name: ____________________**	**37 Pts**

I. Look at pictures and name the school subjects. **6 Pts.**

1.  ______________________
2.  ______________________
3.  ______________________
4.  ______________________
5.  ______________________
6. 

____

II. Fill in the correct question tags. **8 Pts.**

1. You interviewed the Queen, ____________________________
2. I am going to have a party, ___________________________
3. Maths isn't difficult, ____________________________________
4. Your children aren't allergic to milk, ______________________
5. You understand this exercise, ___________________________
6. James doesn't play basketball, __________________________
7. Louisa likes ice cream, ___________________________
8. You must pass this test, _______________________________

III. Fill in the spaces with the correct tense. Past Progressive or simple past? 13 Pts.

1. A group of boys ________________ (to play) pool when a man _____________ (to run) into the activity centre and _____________ (to grab) the money.
2. While our teacher ________________ (to show) us how to play rugby, he ___________ (to fall) and _____________ (to break) his leg.
3. My father couldn't sleep last night. He ________________ (to watch) TV at 4.00am (He started watching TV at 3.45am)
4. The child's mother ______________ (to jump) up when he_____________ (to scream).
5. While the teacher _______________ (to explain) the homework, the girls in the back row______________________ (to chat).
6. It ____________ (to start) to rain while we _____________ (to have) a picnic.

IV. Write the questions for the following answers. 10 Pts.

1. My name is Robert Smith.

   ____ 1 Pt.
2. I come from Canada.

   ____ 2 Pts.
3. I go to school in Montreal.

   ____ 2 Pts.
4. No we don't wear school uniforms.

   ____ 2 Pts.
5. There are six lessons a day.

   ____ 2 Pts.
6. My favourite subject is German.

   ____ 1 Pt.

Extra Practice

1. How do you say **'Schön dich kennen zu lernen'** in English?

   ____

2. Name three verbs from the 'word family' 'to speak'.

   1.______________ 2. _________________3. ____________

3. How do you say '**Wie schade'** in English?

   ____

4.  This is my ________________. I can see when I have maths and when I have PE.

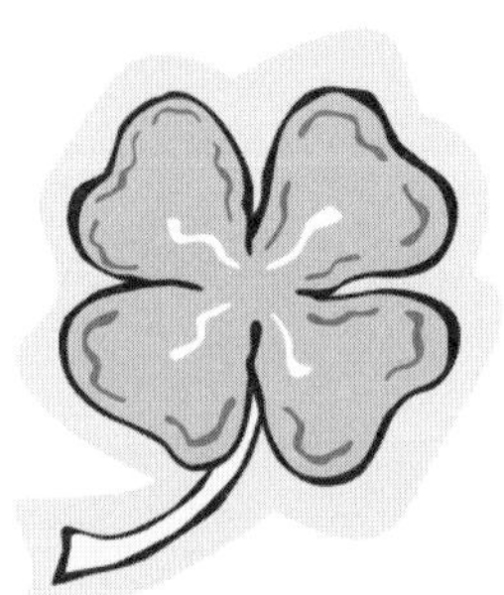

Good luck!

2.2 Short Test 2 – Unit 2

Short Test 2 **Green Line Unit 2**

Your score ____________ **Name: ___________________ 24 Pts.**

I. Please translate the following sentences

Comparatives and Superlatives **12 Pts.**

1. Kevin ist der glücklichste Junge in der Klasse
2. Miley Cyrus ist berühmter al Sarah Connor
3. Ich mag unseren Geschichtslehrer. Er ist der beste Lehrer der ganzen Welt.
4. Wissenschaft ist das schwerste Fach in der Schule.

____

____

____

____

____

____

II. Relative Clauses **12 Pts.**

1. Robin Hood, war ein Mann, der in Sherwood Forest gelebt hat.
2. Mary spricht gerade mit dem Jungen, dessen Mutter aus Amerika kommt.
3. Kaffee ist ein heißes Getränk, das viele Menschen morgens trinken.
4. Ich lese gerade das neue Buch, dass ich gestern im Buchladen kaufte.

____

____

____

____

____

____

____

Extra practice

Prepositions

1. Der kleine Junge rennt seinem Papa entgegen.
2. Das Postamt ist gegenüber des Kinos.
3. Hannah sitzt zwischen Rebecca und Annabelle.
4. Mein Handy fiel mir aus der Tasche.

Vocabulary

1. Wir gingen in die Ausstellung über das Mittelalter in Nottingham.
2. Meine Mama und mein Papa vergleichen ihre Kinder nicht.
3. Alexander Graham Bell erfand das Telefon.
4. Unsere Lehrer organisierten ein Bogenschießturnier an der Schule.

Good luck!

2.3 Short Test 3 – Unit 3

Short Test 3 **Unit 3**

Your score ___________ **Name: __________________** **27 Pts.**

I. Fill in the gaps. Use 'will' or 'going to'. **12 Pts.**

1. I think that Manchester United ____________ win the football match this evening.
2. The Smiths _________________ visit their friends in New York next summer.
3. It _______________ (not) rain at the weekend.
4. Our teacher ___________________ probably give us a lot of homework next weekend.
5. Mary: 'I can't find my pen.'

   Gillian: 'I ______________lend you my pen.'
6. Look at that angry dog! He _________________ bite the lady.
7. I hope we _______________ be on time for the concert.
8. _____Louise ______________spend the night at her friend's house?
9. That man fell off the ladder! I _______________ call the doctor!
10. The weather ______________ be good at Christmas.
11. I want to get a good mark on this test. I __________________ learn my vocabulary every evening this week.
12. __________the children ___________________________spend Christmas Eve with their grandparents?

II. Put the correct preposition in the correct place in the questions. **5 Pts.**

about - for - from - at -to

1. ______ who are you waiting ________?
2. ______ what were the children laughing _______?
3. ______ where does your teacher come________?
4. ______ who did you talk______?
5. ______ what are you looking_______?

III. Vocabulary – fill in the correct word in the gaps. 10 Pts.

1. The fans were disappointed about the football match. The result was nil- nil. (0-0) but ________________ the team didn't lose.
2. It is not nice to _________someone______. You must ask **all** your friends to come to your party.
3. When I __________ I want to be a guitarist in a rock band. I am a child now and I am learning to play the guitar.
4. The concert is tonight. I hope we can go ________________after the concert and get an ___________________from the singer. I have a pen and a piece of paper with me.
5. There were very big ______________at the concert. The music was really loud.
6. I think that Arsenal will win the football match. I am not 100% sure, it is only a ________________.
7. Little Lucy runs away when she sees big dogs. She is ______________________dogs.
8. It takes a long time when Mary telly a story. She tells us all the ______________________ not just the general information.
9. Please __________________ if you want to go to the football match or the concert. You can't go to both.

IV. Extra Practice

Vocabulary: Name three types of food that you can find in a traditional English breakfast.

1. ______________________
2. ______________________
3. ______________________

Good luck!

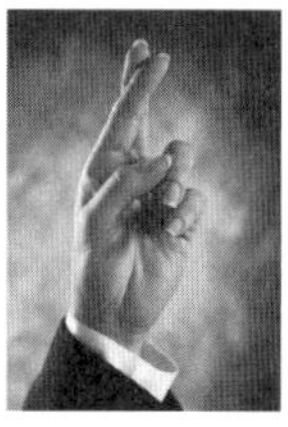

2.4 Short Test 4 - Unit 4

Short Test 4 **Unit 4**

Your score ____________ **Name: ___________________** **32 Pts.**

I. Fill in the table with the missing irregular verbs. **10 Pts.**

infinitive	simple past	past participle
1. to break		
2. to write		
3. to eat		
4. to give		
5. to hit		
6. to leave		
7. to have		
8. to read		
9. to see		
10. to think		

II. Write sentences using the present perfect. **9 Pts.**

1. We __________________ (to be) in London for two days but we ____________ (to see/not) Buckingham Palace yet.
2. George ____________ (to lose) his camera so he can't take any photos.
3. The tour guide _______already ____________ (to show) the group most of the sights.
4. Lucy _______ never __________ (to see) the Alps.
5. How many museums ________ you _______________ (to visit) so far?
6. It is foggy so the plane _______________ (to take off/not) yet.
7. Jack's daughter ________ just ____________ (to come) downstairs with her suitcase.
8. __________ you ______________ (to book) the flights for your next holiday?

III. Simple past or present perfect? Fill in the verbs using the correct tense. 10 Pts.

1. We ________________ (to go) for a walk yesterday afternoon.
2. Where __________you _______________ (to spend) your holiday last summer?
3. The tour group ________________ (to get off/not) the bus because it was raining in London.
4. _________the milkman ____________ (to be) yet?

   Yes, he ________already_________ (to be). There are three pints of milk at the back door.
5. ___________you ever ___________ (to meet) a famous person?
6. My dad ___________ (to speak) to the tour operator ten minutes ago and he said that the plane ____________ (to arrive/not) yet.
7. Mrs Brown ______just____________. She is in the shower.
8. Anna _________________ (to oversleep/not) yesterday morning. She ____________ (to get up) early and ___________ (to pack) her suitcase for the trip.
9. The children are very excited because they _________ never __________ (to be) abroad (im Ausland). They are going to go to Turkey next week.
10. Nancy __________________ (to finish) her homework so she can't go to her friend's house

IV. Short answers. Please fill in the correct short answers. 3 Pts.

1. Have you forgotten your book? Yes, __________
2. Did the teacher answer all the questions? No, __________
3. Do your parents go for a walk every afternoon? Yes, __________
4. Can the children go pony trekking in the city? No, __________
5. Does your dad wash up? Yes, __________
6. Has the rain stopped? No, ___________

Good luck!

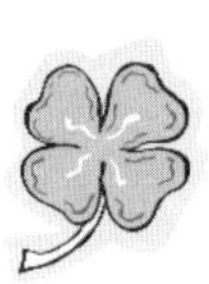

2.5 Short Test 5 – Unit 5

Short Test 5	**Unit 5**
Your score ____________ **Name: ___________________**	**34 Pts.**

I. Philip is talking to Stuart and Rebecca about their plans for the afternoon. Fill in the gaps using the correct form of the verb. 15 Pts

1. Philip: 'If it ______________ (not/rain), we ________________ (go) to the lake.'
2. Stuart: 'That's a good idea. I ______________ (ask) my mum if she __________ (have) time to drive us there.'
3. Philip: 'That would be great.' 'Going in the car is much faster than taking the bus.'
4. Rebecca: 'What ________you ________ (do) if it____________ (rain)?'
5. Stuart: 'If the weather ____________(not/be)good, we ____________ (stay)at home and watch a film, _________(question tag)we Philip.
6. Philip: 'Yes, we___________ (short answer). Rebecca, __________ (ask) your brother if he ________________ (lend)us one of his DVDs.'
7. Rebecca: 'I ___________ (ask) him if he_________ (want) to lend you the film.'
8. Philip: 'Would you like to join us, Rebecca? You can come with us, ____________? (question tag)
9. Rebecca: 'Yes, that would be great. Let's wait and see what the weather will do then!'

II. Fill in the correct form of the modal verbs. Remember to use the substitutes. (Ersatzformen) **19 Pts**

can – may - must - need
have to
can't - may not – mustn't – needn't

1. The children ____________________ study this evening. There is no school tomorrow.
2. My dad ________________ drive me to school yesterday morning because he was ill. I ___________________ walk.
3. It is very cold in the winter. We _____________ wear hats and gloves. In the summer we ________________ wear hats and gloves.
4. Ronald ______________________ go out yesterday. His mum said he _________________ stay at home and do his homework.
5. If you finish your homework today, you _____________ do any homework at the weekend.
6. The children ______________________ speak English before they started school. Now they _______________ speak English very well.
7. Louise didn't finish writing the letter before she went to bed because she was too tired. She _____________________ finish it tomorrow morning.
8. You ___________ write on your desk. It is forbidden.
9. When I was four years old I _____________ ride a bike. Now I ____________ ski and when I am older I __________________ to drive a car.
10. My best friend hopes he __________________ come to the concert next weekend too. He ________________ ask his mum first.
11. '____________ I borrow your bike, Dad? My wheel is broken.'
    'No, you ________________. I need my bike. I want to go to the library'.
12. Kate __________________ tidy her room yesterday. Her mum tidied it for her.

III. Vocabulary (Extra practice)

Please fill in the correct word.

1. When someone is old and can't live at home. He /she can live in an ________________________________.
2. We have got a new ______________________________ this term. I have got maths on Monday, Wednesday and Friday. I have only got PE once.
3. We were so bored yesterday. We ____________________ all day with nothing to do.
4. How long does it _________________ you to get to school?
5. Most 10 year old don't _______________________ in Father Christmas. 
6. How long is the _________________ to America? Do you have to fly for a long time?
7. Most teenager ______________ with their friends at weekends. They prefer spending time with their friends and not with their parents.
8. I am __________________ when I am watching a _______________ film. (langweilig sein /gelangweilt)

Good luck!

2.6 Short Test 6 – Unit 6

Short Test 6		**Unit 6**
Your score ___________	**Name:** __________________	**26 Pts.**

I. Choose the correct answer. Cross out the wrong words. **8 Pts.**

James arrived home last night and wanted **everything/something** to eat. He was hungry! He looked in the fridge and saw that **somebody/anybody** had eaten all the food. There was **anything/nothing** left. James called his mum but **nobody/anybody** answered. Where was she? **Anything/Something** was wrong! James went upstairs to look for his mum but she wasn't there. He looked **anywhere/ everywhere** but he couldn't find her. She is always home in the evenings! James had **no/every** idea where his mum was. James decided to call his neighbor to ask if she had seen James' mum **somewhere/anywhere**, but he couldn't find his phone! **Something/Anything** was strange! **Nothing/everything** was normal **No/Any** food, **no/any** mum! Then he noticed **something/anything** on the floor. He picked it up! It was a note from his mum. It said:

Dear James,

I am at the supermarket. We haven't got **some/any** *food left. You can order* **something/everything** *from the pizzeria if you are hungry. I won't be long.*

I will be back soon. There is **nothing/ anything** *to worry about.*

See you soon.

Love mum

PS Your mobile phone is in the drawer in your bedroom.

II. Rewrite the sentences using 'no', 'nobody', 'nowhere', and 'nothing'. **8 Pts.**

1. Dad doesn't know anything about the surprise party.

____

2. We didn't see anybody in the shop.

____

3. Christopher doesn't go anywhere at the weekends.

____

4. There aren't any problems with the homework.

____

III. What are the opposites of the following words? **4 Pts.**

1. to push ↔ ____________________
2. thin ↔ ____________________
3. to be born ↔ ____________________
4. to stay the same ↔ ____________________

IV. Can you translate the following verbs? **6 Pts.**

1. teilnehmen ____________________
2. sich beschweren ____________________
3. sich freuen auf ____________________
4. erwarten ____________________
5. loswerden ____________________
6. nicht einverstanden sein ____________________

Good luck!

2.1 Short Test 7 - Unit 7

Short Test 7		**Unit 7**
Your score ____________	**Name: ___________________**	**34 Pts.**

I. Change the adjectives into adverbs. **8 Pts.**

1. loud ____________________
2. quiet ____________________
3. cheerful ____________________
4. good ____________________
5. dangerous ____________________
6. angry ____________________
7. simple ____________________
8. fast ____________________

II. Adjective or adverb? Fill in the gaps with the correct form of the word. **14 Pts.**

1. Tony works very ________________ (hard). He does his homework ___________ (perfect). He is an ________________ (excellent) pupil.
2. Most children feel ________________ (wonderful) when they answer all the questions________________ (correct).
3. The ski trip was ________________ (good). Everything went really ________________ (good).
4. You can do this exercise ________________. (easy) Just answer all the questions ________________ (careful).
5. Mike is a_________ (bad) driver. He drives much too ________________ (fast) and doesn't watch the road ________________ .(proper) (genau/richtig)
6. The children are playing ________________. (noisy) They are having fun and dancing ________________ (wild).

III. Please fill in the correct of the adjectives to make comparisons. **4 Pts.**

1. Our football team played as ________________ (good) as the other team.
2. The old man walked ____________________________ (slow) than his young grandson did.
3. Your idea sounds _____________ (good) than my idea.
4. Newsreaders (Nachrichtensprecher/-innen) speak more _________________ (clear) than most people do.

IV. Vocabulary. Please match the words to the correct definitions. Please write the correct words in the spaces. **8 Pts.**

1. something or someone that we are not able to see _______________
2. the top person in a group__________________
3. a place where you can borrow books, CDs, DVDs and magazines from ___________________
4. something/someone whose style is new, not old fashioned ______________________
5. to know someone or something because you have seen him/her/it before _______________________
6. the opposite of to begin or to start _____________________
7. to repair something ___________________________
8. someone who is gentle and caring, helpful to others _____________________

a) to end
b) modern
c) to mend
d) library
e) kind
f) invisible
g) chief
h) to recognize

V. Extra Practice

What are these things?

1.  ______________________________

2.  ______________________________

3.  ______________________________

4.  ______________________________

5.  ______________________________

6.  ______________________________

Good luck!

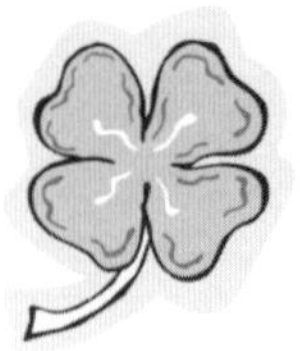

2.2 Schulaufgabe 1-1

Written English Test 1 **Unit 1**

Your score ____________ **Name: ____________________ 75 Pts.**

I. Complete the dialogue with question tags and short answers. **19 Pts.**

Andrew is talking to his daughter Emily.

Andrew: You've got a new girl in your class, _______________?

Emily: Yes, ____________. Her name is Sabine. It's a nice name, ____________? She comes from Germany.

Andrew: You can't speak German, ___________?

Emily: No, ______________but Sabine speaks English. German school children learn English at school in Germany, ______________?

Andrew: Yes, ______________. You visited Germany when you were three, ______________? You remember that holiday, ______________?

Emily: Yes, _______________. It was great fun, _____________________?

Andrew: Yes, _____________. Mum and I loved the food, ___________? You didn't like those white sausages, _____________?

Emily: I can't remember that Dad, __________? I was only three, _____________?

Andrew: That's true. You remember the big swimming pool in the hotel, _______________?

Emily: Yes, I do. The water wasn't very warm, ______________?
Dad, I think Sabine misses Germany, _________________?

Andrew: Yes, I am sure she does.

II. Fill in the sentences using 'while' or 'when' and the correct form of the verb. Simple past or past progressive. 13 Pts

1. _________ Louise _______________________ (to work) in the garden, the doorbell rang.
2. The children were waiting for the bus _________ the cars ________________ .(to crash)
3. The burglar broke into the sports centre __________ the team ______________ (to play) football outside.
4. My mum cried with joy ________ I _________ (to show) her my 'A' in English.
5. The boys started laughing ________ Mary ________________ (to read) aloud.
6. We were playing rugby in PE __________ Richard _________ (to fall) and _________ (to break) his leg.

III. Vocabulary - Fill in the gaps with the correct verb. Put the verb into the correct tense where possible. 8 Pts.

1. The opposite of 'to like' is ____________________.
2. I like chocolate ice cream more than vanilla ice cream. I ___________ chocolate ice cream.
3. James hit the ball back to his partner yesterday. He _______________ the ball during the tennis match.
4. Nick throws the ball to his dog and he ________________ it in his mouth.
5. You think Manchester United is a good team. I think Manchester United is a good team. We ______________ that Manchester United is a good team.
6. If you don't understand a word, you must ________ it _______ in a dictionary.
7. When I say, 'Would you like a drink? I ________________ you a drink.
8. My sister can't find her book. She must ______________ it.

IV. Vocabulary –mixed bag 6 Pts.
Fill in the gaps with the correct word or phrase.

1. When somebody sneezes, we say '___________ '.
2. _____________ is my favourite subject. I like learning about the past.
3. We use 'to be going to' when we are talking about the _____________.
4. These are ____________. We use them to play table tennis.

5. My older cousin gives me her clothes. My clothes are not new. They are ________________.
6. The weather is not nice at the moment. It is cold and wet. It is ______________.

VI. Can you name the after school activities? **4 Pts.**

V. Sabine is writing to her friend in Berlin about her new school in England. Read the letter and answer the questions.

Dear Stephie,

How are you? I hope that you are fine.
My new school is great. The other children in my class are very friendly. It is a big class. There are sixteen boys and seventeen girls. I sit next to a very nice girl. Her name is Divia. She comes from India. She is new too. She came to England two months ago.
School starts at 9.00am and finishes at 3.30pm. It is a long day but we don't have much homework. My favourite subject is geography. You like geography too, don't you? I also like maths but it is sometimes difficult.
There are a lot of after school activities at my school. I joined drama club three weeks ago. It is great fun. We are going to do a musical this year and I am going to sing a solo. I am very excited. Last week I sang for the first time in front of the group and everybody clapped and cheered. Is there a drama club at your school?
I am also going to join the table tennis club. I need to do some exercise and table tennis is good fun. There is also a nice boy in the table tennis club. I like him a lot. He looks like Harry from the group One Direction. His name is Paul.
We are going to have a Halloween party next week. Everybody is going to dress up as ghosts or witches. We are going to make some jack -'o-lanterns out of pumpkins in art class. We are going to have a competition to see who has the scariest jack -'o-lantern. The winner is going to get a prize. Do you celebrate Halloween in Berlin?
I miss you a lot Stephie and I hope you can come to England and visit me soon.
Please write back soon.

Love,

Sabine

VII. True or false- if the answer is false, please write the correct answer in the line below. 17 Pts.

1. Sabine lives in Berlin. True False

___

2. Laura comes from India. True False

___

3. Sabine doesn't like her new school. True False

___

4. The children aren't very friendly. True False

___

5. Sabine is going to sing on her own in the musical. True False

___

6. All of the other children in the drama group laughed when Sabine sang in front of the group. True False

___

7. Harry from 'One Direction' is in Sabine's table tennis club. True False

___

8. Sabine is going to go to a Halloween party next week. True False

___

9. The children are going to make jack -'o-lanterns out of turnips. True False

___

10. Sabine doesn't want Stephie to visit her in England. True False

___

VIII. Look the text and find an example of- please underline your examples. 8 Pts.

1. the simple past
2. the simple present
3. the going to future
4. a question tag

Good luck!

2.3 Schulaufgabe 1-2

Written English Test 2 **Unit 2**

Your score ____________ **Name: ___________________** **80 Pts.**

I. Please write the numbers. **8 Pts.**

2,356	
16,608	
12,457,911	
1,815,501	

II. Comparisons and superlatives. **10 Pts.**
Fill in the gaps with the correct form of the adjective.

1. Jenny's dad is ___________ (old) than your dad.
2. Sam can run very fast. He is the __________ (fast) runner in our school.
3. Driving slowly is ___________ (safe) than driving fast.
4. This food is disgusting. It is the __________ (bad) food I have ever eaten.
5. My boots were __________________ (expensive) than my mum's boots.
6. Andrew is ___________ (good) at science than his sister.
7. Lady Gaga is ________________ (popular) in America than Jeanette Biedermann.
8. That crossing is really dangerous. I think it is the ________________ (dangerous) crossing in the town.
9. Learning English is ___________ (easy) than learning German.
10. People say that dolphins  are _____________ (clever) than sharks. 

III. Write the sentences using 'as…as' or 'as not…as' from the information in the German sentences below. **8 Pts.**

1. Mein Schreibtisch ist genauso aufgeräumt wie dein Schreibtisch.

____

2. Marys Haare sind nicht so lang wie Emilys Haare.

____

3. Ein Mercedes ist genauso teuer wie ein BMW.

____

4. Zuhause zu essen ist nicht so teuer wie in einem Restaurant zu essen.

____

IV. Fill in the correct relative pronoun. Do not use 'that'. **6 Pts.**

1. The woman __________I saw at the cinema is my mum's best friend.
2. The book __________we read a school last term was very interesting.
3. I found a ring _________was very expensive.
4. The old man __________dog died last week is very sad. .
5. I have lost the mobile phone _________I bought last month.
6. Anna likes the boys _________ are in One Direction.

V. Put the two sentences together. Use a relative clause only if you need one! Do **not** use 'that'. **16 Pts.**

1. We went to the theatre. It has an excellent sound system.
2. Do you know the boy? He joined the table tennis club last week.
3. The boy is in my class. We always see him at the bus stop.
4. Is the woman your aunt? You are talking to her.
5. I have got a CD. My sister wants to borrow it.
6. There is a computer in the classroom. Its hard drive is broken.
7. The school won an award (eine Auszeichnung) for its history course. I went to it.
8. The house has got a very big living room. She lives in it.

VI. Vocabulary - Fill in the correct word. **12 Pts.**

1. The opposite of in the beginning is ______________________.
2. Another word for every day is _________.
3. Somebody who is 'nett' and 'freundlich' is ____________.
4. I say 'John is bigger than Michael'. I am ____________ John and Michael.
5. I can look up words in a dictionary. A dictionary is very ____________.
6. The opposite of a friend is an ____________.
7. The man took the money that didn't belong to him. He ___________ the money.
8. The mother hen ___________ the chicks from the wolf.
9.  The pizza is ____ the box. There is also a piece of pizza _________ the box.
10.  The people are ____________ the number 10. The number 10 is _________ the people.

VII. You learned a lot about Robin Hood in Unit 2. Can you answer the questions about Robin Hood? Please write your answers in full sentences. 20 Pts.

1. Was Robin Hood a famous outlaw or a famous king?

___

2. Who did Robin Hood love?

___

3. Was 'Little John' a big man or a small man?

___

4. Where did Robin Hood live?

___

5. Are the Sheriff of Nottingham and Robin Hood good friends?

___

6. Who did Robin Hood steal money from?

___

7. Who did Robin Hood give the money to?

___

8. Which outlaw had the biggest appetite?

___

9. Were the Merry Men Robin Hood's friends or enemies?

___

10. What weapon did Robin Hood use? 

___

Good luck!

2.4 Schulaufgabe 2-1

Written English Test 3		**Units 1-3**
Your score ___________	**Name: __________________**	**70 Pts.**

Reading Comprehension

Safety at Concerts.

Going to a concert and listening to a fantastic singer or band is great fun. You can listen to the music, dance and sing along to your favourite songs. You can see your favourite pop stars in real life! Lots of teenagers like going to concerts with their friends and have a lot of fun there.

Concerts are always very crowded. It is important to follow some basic rules and keep safe at concerts.

Firstly, it is often very hot at concerts because there are so many people there. Always wear light clothes so that you don't overheat. You will be too hot in a big winter jacket. It is also important to drink a lot of water so that you don't dehydrate (dehydrieren). You should eat a good meal before you go so that you are not hungry at the concert. The food at concerts is often expensive and the queues are long. You don't want to feel dizzy at the concert and miss all the fun!

You don't know the people at concerts. You have to be careful. There are often pick pockets at concerts who try to steal people's money. Make sure you have your money in a safe place so that no-one can steal it. Boys-don't put your wallets in your back pockets.

Some people drink alcohol at concerts. If you see people who are drunk and 'rowdy', move away. Don't stand next to them.

You should never be alone at a concert. Always stay with your friends even when you go to the toilet. In America this is called the 'buddy system'. It is much safer to stay together.

If you are frightened or don't feel well you can always go to a security guard. They will help you.

I. **Please answer the questions about the text. Please write your answers in full sentences.** **16 Pts.**

1. What can you do at a concert? **(3)**

____

____

2. Are concerts always safe? **(1)**

____

3. Name three things you must do at a concert so that you don't get dizzy. **(6)**

   1. _______________________________
   2. _______________________________
   3. _______________________________

4. What is a 'pick pocket'? **(2)**

____

5. You haven't learned the word 'rowdy' yet. What do you think it means? Tick the correct answer. **(1)**

   ○ Someone who is crazy and wild?

   ○ Someone who is quiet and peaceful?

6. What is the 'buddy system'? **(3)**

____

____

II. Fill in the correct form of the 'going to' or 'will' future with the verb in bracket. 16 Pts

It is a hot summer's day and the children are happy. It is the school holidays! Six weeks of getting up late, swimming, meeting friends, going to bed late and just having fun!

Tony is in a great mood. He is meeting friends at the pool today. He is chatting to his mum about his plans.

Tony: 'Mum, I ________________ (to go) to the pool and I am going to meet Julian, Mike and Andrew there too. I think the girls from our class ____________ (to meet) us there too.

Mum: OK Tony, who ___________ (to drive) you there? I can't today I have a doctor's appointment.

Tony: 'Oh, I didn't know that. I _______________ (to phone) Andrew and see if his mum can drive.

Mum: Alright Tony. Let me know. I ________________ (to leave) in half an hour.

10 minutes later

Tony: 'Mum, it is all organized. Andrew's mum _______________ (to drive) us to the pool and we _______________________ (to take) the bus home.

Mum: 'Oh good. That is great. I _________________ (to drive) you next time. Have you got any food and a drink?

Tony: No, I _______________ (to buy) something there.

Mum: 'Tony, it is so expensive at the pool. At least take a drink.'

Tony: 'OK, I ________________ (to take) a drink. It _____________ (to be) hot all day today. I _____________ probably _____________ (to be) really thirsty.

Mum: 'Yes, take two bottles of water. There is some in the kitchen. I___________________ (to go) shopping after the doctor's and I can buy some more. Take some fruit too.

Tony: 'OK Mum, but I ________________ (to buy) some chips as well. I don't just want healthy fruit!

Mum: I must leave now. Oh my goodness! Look at the time I ______________ (to be) late. Enjoy your day. The weather forecast said it ________________ (to rain) tomorrow!

III. Verbs and prepositions. Write questions based on the underlined words. (Be careful of the position of the preposition and the verb) **8 Pts**

1. Uncle Peter tripped over *(stolpern über)* the bag that was on the floor.

____?

2. My daughter is going to ask the teacher for some extra exercises.

____?

3. We were listening to the new CD when the CD player broke.

____?

4. Mary stays with her grandmother at Christmas.

____?

IV. Vocabulary. Read the descriptions (Beschreibungen) and fill in the correct word. **6 Pts**

1. When I plan to do something, it is my ________________ to do it.
2. Another word for two times is______________.
3. Somebody who has a cold or the flu is ___________.
4. A person who plays the guitar in a band is the______________.
5. When I am a little angry I feel__________________.
6. When a new person joins our class and the teacher tells us his/her name. This is to

   ________________ a new person.

V. Can you explain the following words? **4 Pts.**

1. What is a puppy?

   ____

2. What is a leader?

   ____

VI. Please translate the following sentences. **12 Pts**

1. Der Mann torkelt herum. Ich glaube dass er zu viel Bier getrunken hat.

 ____

 ____

2. Was für eine Woche! Heute Abend werde ich wahrscheinlich früh ins Bett gehen.

 ____

 ____

3. Es ist wirklich ärgerlich. Mein kleiner Bruder hat meine Lautsprecher kaputtgemacht gestern.

 ____

 ____

4. Willst du (Schinken-)Speck und Eier oder Toast und Marmelade zum Frühstuck. Entscheide dich, bitte.

 ____

 ____

VII. Mixed Bag. There is one mistake in each sentence below. Can you find the mistake and correct it. Write the correct sentence on the line below. **8 Pts.**

1. The drummer plays a guitar in a band.

 ____

2. I hope the sun will shines tomorrow.

 ____

3. Next summer The Smiths going to visit China.

 ____

4. Look the sun is coming out. It will stop raining!

 ____

5. For who are you waiting?

 ____

6. I am really happy I got a 6 in maths. (→Du bist bestimmt nicht glücklich!)

 ____

7. 'Ladys and gentleman, the show will begin in ten minutes.'

 ____

8. When Simon grows, he wants to be a fireman.

 ____

2.5 Schulaufgabe 2-2

Written English Test 4		**Units 1-4**
Your score ____________	**Name:** ____________________	**86 Pts.**

I. Dictation. The dictation is in the answer key. **20 Pts.**

____

____

____

____

____

____

____

____

____

____

____

____

____

____

____

____

____

____

____

II. What are the opposites of the following words? **5 Pts.**

1. mountain ≠ ____________________
2. cheap ≠ ____________________
3. after ≠ ____________________
4. to take off (a T-shirt) ≠ ____________________
5. wife ≠ ____________________

III. Can you explain the following words? **8 Pts**

1. What is a milkman?

___

2. What is a scrapbook?

___

3. What is a nurse?

___

4. What is a weather forecast?

___

IV. Look at the pictures. Can you fill in the correct 'moving' verb? **4 Pts**

1. The girl is ______________ the bus.

2. The man is ______________ the trolley. (Einkaufswagen)

3. The family is ______________ on the beach.

4. The dog is ______________ the frisbee.

V. Please translate the verbs and then fill in the correct forms. **9 Pts.**

German	English - infinitive	simple past	past participle
1. werden			
2. sich fühlen			
3. schlagen			
4. verlieren			
5. stehlen			
6. tragen			

VI. Present perfect or simple past? Write in the correct form of the verb in the following sentences. (Underline the key words- it helps!) 14 Pts.

1. It is 10.00am and my dad ____________just ____________ (to come) downstairs. He usually gets up earlier but he ______________ (to stay up) very late last night.
2. When _____________ you ____________ (to tidy up) up your bedroom? It looks great.
3. Last week we ______________ (to go) to the travel agent's and _____________ (to buy) some plane tickets for our trip to London.
4. _________your teacher _____________ (to correct) the test yet?
5. Our guests form America ___________________ (to be/not) to Munich yet.
6. Unfortunately my mum ________________________ (to buy/not) me a new mobile phone last Christmas. She said it was too expensive.
7. The smugglers ____________already ______________ (to hide) the treasure. They put it on their boat yesterday.
8. How many times ___________your best friend _______________ (to stay) at your house so far?
9. Auntie Mary's children ___________never _____________ (to visit) to New York. They want to go next summer.
10. We __________________ (to leave/not) the cinema an hour ago. We __________just ______________ (to leave).

VII. Tense check - read the sentences and <u>correct the mistakes</u>. Write the correct sentence on the line below. 6 Pts.

1. Did you forgot to do the homework yesterday?

____

2. I did five questions so far.

____

3. Sylvia haven't packed the suitcase yet.

____

4. Nicolas is going to booking a holiday next month.

____

5. The smugglers always looks for a good place to hide the treasure.

____

6. We did pay a lot of money for the hotel last summer.

____

VIII. Writing. **20 Pts.**

You are an English boy/girl who is on holiday in Munich visiting your pen friend. Write a postcard to your parents and tell them about your holiday. Make sure you write about:

- the city of Munich
- the weather
- your pen friend's family
- what you have seen/done so far
- what you are going to do tomorrow
- if you are having fun

Good luck!

2.6 Schulaufgabe 3-1

Written English Test 5		**Units 1- 5**
Your score ___________	**Name: _______________**	**84 Pts.**

I. Mothering Sunday. **18 Pts.**

Mothering Sunday is a day when we celebrate with our mothers and say thank you for everything that they do for us. A lot of people give their mums flowers or chocolates and make special cards for them. Most mums like things that their children make for them.

Mothering Sunday is celebrated in England on the fourth Sunday in Lent (die Fastenzeit), so date changes every year. It is different in Germany, Mothering Sunday is always celebrated on the second Sunday in May. Mothering Sunday is called Mother's Day in America and celebrated on the same day as in Germany.

It is believed that Mothering Sunday goes back to the ancient Greek times when the people celebrated the Mother of the Gods and Goddesses. The Romans also celebrated their mother Goddess Cybele. In Britain it was traditionally a day when the servants (die Diener/Diennerinnen) could go home and visit their mothers. They often picked flowers and took them home to their mums. The fasting rules that people have during Lent were often relaxed that day so the families could enjoy cake together. A traditional cake which was eaten on Mothering Sunday was simnel cake.

All over the world Mothering Sunday is celebrated in different ways and with different traditions. It does not matter how we celebrate but perhaps the things that mums enjoy the most is if they can relax and their children (young or old) help them. It is a day when mothers should be spoiled (verwöhnt)!

Please answer the questions about the text in full sentences.

1. What is Mothering Sunday?

____

2. What do people give their mums on Mothering Sunday?

____

3. When is Mothering Sunday in Britain?

____

4. Is Mothering Sunday an old or a new celebration?

____

5. Could servants visit their mum's on Mothering Sunday?

____

6. How do you celebrate Mothering Sunday?

____

II. Choose the correct word in the sentences below. Cross the wrong word out. 6 Pts.

1. My dog never stops eating and is fat. He is **overweight / too thin**.
2. When American students are 18, they often go to **elementary school/college**.
3. The film about the weather was really **boring / bored**.
4. You must ask your mum for **permission / obligation** to go to the disco.
5. A synonym for 'sad' is **happy / unhappy**.
6. We don't think our teachers **should / shouldn't** give us a lot of homework!

III. Fill in the gaps and make correct 'if' or 'when' sentences. Translate the German word/phrases into English words/phrases. 25 Pts

1. If John _______________ (to go) to America, he _________________ (müssen) learn some new words. American English is a little different to British English.
2. The children ______________ (nicht müssen) go to summer school if they _________ (to pass) their tests.
3. If you ____________ (to call) someone a ___________ (Trottel), he/she ____________ (to find/not) it funny!
4. Passengers can ___________ (to print) their own _____________ (Bordkarten) if they __________ (einchecken) online. It is quick and easy.
5. It is hot today. When Christopher _________ (to arrive) at school today, he _________ (to take off) his _________ (Mantel).
6. We ___________ (to plant/not) the flowers if it ____________ (to stop/not) raining.
7. The students can _____________ (Geld aufbringen) for poor children in India if they _____________ (to have) a ___________ (Bazar).
8. If your friends ___________ (to tell) you to do something ____________ (verrückt), __________ (to do/not) it!
9. If Mary ____________ (to lose) her____________ (Ohrringe), she will be sad.
10. If the train is _______________ (verspätet), David's mum _____________ (to drive) us to school.

IV. **British or American English. Fill in gaps with the correct word.** **8 Pts.**

Keks	1. ________________	5. ________________
Abfall, Müll	2. ________________	6. ________________
Stundenplan	3. ________________	7. ________________
Mathematik	4. ________________	8. ________________

V. Fill in the gaps with 'if' or 'when' in the following sentences. **4 Pts.**

1. ______I win the lottery, I will buy a villa in Spain.
2. ______Mike finishes the test, he will leave the class room.
3. I think we will go to the beach ______is the weather is nice tomorrow.
4. The children can tidy their rooms ______ they get home from school.

VI. Fill in the table with the correct form of the missing modal verbs so that the meaning is the same but the tense is different. **10 Pts.**

present	past	future
He **can /is able to** ride a bike.	He ______________ ride a bike.	He ______________ ride a bike.
The boys ______________ ___________ play football in the park.	The boys **were allowed to** play football in the park.	The boys _____ _____ play football in the park.
All the students ___________ _________ take the test.	All the students ________ _______ take the test.	All the students **will have to** take the test.
The visitors ____________ walk on the grass.	The visitors **aren't allowed to** walk on the grass.	The visitors _____________ walk on the grass.
You **don't have to** answer all the questions.	You ____________________ answer all the questions.	You ____________________ answer all the questions.

VII. Modal verbs – Please translate the following sentences. Pay attention to modal verbs. 13 Pts.

1. Stuart durfte nicht neben seinem Bruder sitzen.

   ____

2. Im nächsten Jahr wird Zoe mit ihrer Freundin in Urlaub fahren dürfen. (3 Pts.)

   ____

3. Mein Papa musste gestern nicht arbeiten.

   ____

4. Das Baby muss Milch trinken.

   ____

5. Paul konnte Englisch sprechen als er fünf war.

   ____

6. Louise wird im nächsten Sommer schwimmen können.

   ____

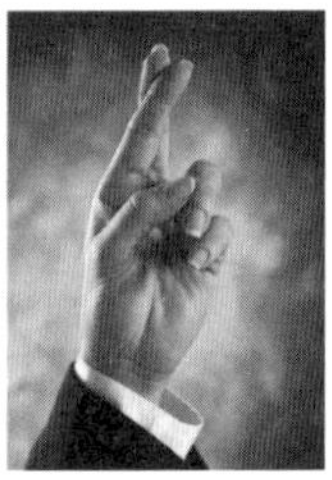

Good luck!

Good luck!

2.7 Schulaufgabe 3-2

Written English Test 3-2		Units 1- 6
Your score ___________	Name: _________________	72 Pts.

Neuschwanstein

Neuschwanstein was built by King Ludwig II. It is known as the castle of the Fairy Tale King. Construction work began in 1869. It was opened to the public in 1886 after King Ludwig's sudden and mysterious death at the age of 41. King Ludwig II only slept in the castle for eleven nights. It was designed by Christian Jank who was a theatrical designer but not an architect. Neuschwanstein means New Swan Stone. The name comes from one of Richard Wagner's opera characters, Swan Knight.

It is one of the most popular places to visit in Germany. There are about 6,000 visitors a day in the summer and about 1.3 million visitors a year. It is one of the most photographed buildings in the world. You can only take photographs of the outside of the castle, it is forbidden to take photographs of the interior of the building.

The castle is located in southwest Bavaria with amazing views of the Alps. It is open daily except Christmas Eve, Christmas Day, New Years Eve, and New Years Day. Tickets are sold from 8.00am to 5.00pm (from April to September) and 9.00am to 3.00pm (from October to March). There are guided tours available in German and English. Tickets costs about €12.

You can walk, take a bus or go in a horse drawn carriage  up to the castle.

I. Read about Neuschwanstein. **16 Pts.**

True or false? Tick the correct box. If the answer is false please write the correct answer on the line below.

1. King Ludwig II started building Neuschwanstein in 1869. True ☐ False ☐

____

2. King Ludwig II lived to be an old man. True ☐ False ☐

____

3. King Ludwig didn't sleep in the castle very often. True ☐ False ☐

____

4. Christian Jank was a famous architect. True ☐ False ☐

____

5. Neuschwanstein means Swan Knight. True ☐ False ☐

____

6. There are about 1.3 million visitors to Neuschwanstein a day in the summer.
True ☐ False ☐

____

7. Visitors are allowed to take photographs of the outside of the castle but not of the inside. True ☐ False ☐

____

8. The castle is never closed to the public. True ☐ False ☐

____

9. Visitors who can speak German or English can go on a guided tour of the castle.
True ☐ False ☐

____

10. You can only get to the castle by bus or by horse drawn carriage.
True ☐ False ☐

____

II. Fill in the blanks with the correct words from the box below. **14 Pts.**

someone (somebody)	anyone (anybody)	everyone (everybody)	no one (nobody)
something	anything	everything	nothing
somewhere	anywhere	everywhere	nowhere

1. Would you like ________________ to eat?
2. Mary lost her handbag ________________ in the city.
3. We can't find ________________ in the book about 'ranches'
4. Don't go ________________ without your mum and dad.
5. ________________ has to help clean up after the party.
6. There is ________________ at school during the summer holidays.
7. We looked ________________ but we couldn't find the keys.
8. There was ________________ interesting on TV last night so we went to the cinema.
9. You can eat and drink ________________ you want in on an all-inclusive holiday.
10. I don't want to go ________________ this evening. I want to sit at home and read a book.
11. ________________ has eaten all the cupcakes. There are none left.
12. My children don't help me in the kitchen. I have to do ________________.
13. Is there ________________ at the ticket office? I need to buy a train ticket.
14. Mr Smith has worked at the company for thirty years. He knows ________________ who works here.

III. Rewrite the sentences below using nobody, nothing, or nowhere. **6 Pts.**

1. Our teacher can't show anyone the answers to the test.

____

2. We didn't go anywhere last weekend.

____

3. We haven't got anything to eat.

____

IV. A day on the ranch. Look at the pictures and write the correct words. **6 Pts.**

1.  **h**________ **r**___________

2.  **b**_____________ **b** _______________

3.  **t**____________

4.  **s**_____________

5.  **s**______________

6.  **c** ______________

V. Translate the verbs and put them in the correct tense. **10 Pts.**

1. All the students ______________________ (teilnehmen an) the school play next month. I hope it _________________ (sein) good.
2. Don't ______________(sich beschweren, sich beklagen) about the homework.
3. The teacher always _____________ (teilen) the gym into two parts so that two classes can have PE at the same time.
4. The teacher __________________ (nicht erkennen, nicht realisieren) that we had a double lesson and let us leave early yesterday.
5. Jim can't ___________________ (los werden) his cold. He has been ill for weeks!
6. The kindergarten children are really happy at the moment. They _______________________________ (sich freuen auf) going to school.
7. The boy over there ____________ just _____________ (treten) his little brother and now he is crying.
8. The big dog _________________ (erschreckte) the small children when he barked loudly.
9. Children never ______________ (einverstanden sein) with their parents about what time they should go to bed.

VI. Mediation- please mediate a conversation between Lucy and Danny. **20 Pts.**

Lucy has a visitor from America, her American friend, Danny. Lucy welcomes him to the farm and asks him if he wants to look around the stables. Danny thanks Lucy and tells her that he likes horses a lot. He asks if they can go horse riding. Lucy agrees and says that she will get the saddles. She says that must inform her mum before they ride around the farm. Danny tells Lucy that he lives on a big ranch in America where they have got a lot of cattle. Lucy asks if she can visit him one day because they have recently learned about America at school. She asks Danny if he can square dance. Danny says that he can square dance and suggests that Lucy visits him in America next summer to take part in the cattle drive with the cowboys. Lucy is really pleased and asks Danny to teach her how to square dance. He agrees.

Good luck!

2.8 Schulaufgabe 4-1

Written English Test 4		**Units 1- 7**
Your score ______________	**Name:** ___________________	**70 Pts.**

I. What are the English words? **6 Pts.**

1. jedoch ____________________________
2. Märchen ____________________________
3. Blatt ____________________________
4. unsichtbar ____________________________
5. Zauberer ____________________________
6. Stiefschwester ____________________________

II. Translate the verbs and fill in the gaps below. Use the correct form. **8 Pts.**

vorschlagen, beten, verbessern, flicken,
sich verlieben, erkennen, zittern, sich benehmen

1. When we are at church we have to _____________. We cannot chat and laugh.
2. It is good that Jim is a boy scout. He knows how to _____________a tent.
3. Romeo and Juliet is a famous story about a man and women who ______________ _______________.
4. A lot of young people go to England because they want to _____________ their English. They want to speak English better.
5. Our teacher dyed (färben) her hair. It was blond but now it is black. We didn't ________________ her when she came into the classroom. We thought we had a new teacher.
6. If you are at a restaurant and don't know what to eat you can ask the waiter to _______________ something. He can give you an idea about what to have.
7. The little boy started to _____________ when he saw the big, black dog. He is frightened of dogs.
8. The priest asked us to _____________ for the people who died in the fire.

III. Adjective or adverb? Fill in the gap with the correct form. **8 Pts.**

1. Catherine and Bella have known each other for ten years. They know each other really______________. (good)
2. Catherine lives in Williamsburg, America and Bella lives in Munich, Germany. They don't meet very often but they talk on the telephone______________. (regular)
3. Once Catherine came to Germany to visit Bella. They had a really ______________ (good) time.
4. Catherine found it difficult to understand German but Bella translated each sentence very ______________. (careful)
5. It was the middle of August but the weather was still ______________. (terrible)
6. The girls couldn't go swimming because the water in the pool was too ______________ (cold)
7. The spent most of their time hanging out with Bella's friends. Catherine learned how to speak German ______________. (quick)
8. Catherine felt ______________ (happy) in Germany and would like to come and visit again soon.

IV. Use the words in the box to fill in the gaps. Be careful you may need to use the comparative adverb form. **10 Pts.**

dangerous - beautiful – fast – quiet – logical – energetic – bad – boring - serious-sleepy

1. Little Catherine was very tired this morning. She couldn't open her eyes. She got up and brushed her teeth____________________.
2. The ballet dancer is excellent. She can dance ____________________ *than* anyone I know.
3. Our neighbour isn't *as* ____________________*as* my dad. He makes jokes all the time.
4. The new maths teacher explains the material ____________________ *than* the teacher we had before. I understand it now.
5. The young man who lives next to us drives like a mad man. He drives more ____________________*than* anyone in the street.
6. The cleaning lady cleaned the house ____________________*than* my mum. She has got so much power!
7. Boys can't whisper *as* ____________________*as* girls.  They are always too loud.
8. A horse can run ____________________*than* a donkey. 
9. The children's dad's cooking is really bad. . He cooks ____________________ than anyone in the family.
10. I hope this exercise wasn't too ____________________!

V. Translation- please translate the following sentences. **18 Pts.**

1. In Märchen ist die Stiefmutter oft eine grausame Frau.

____

____

2. Glaubst du, dass es am Ende eines Regenbogens einen Schatz gibt?

____

____

3. Das Essen meiner Mutter schmeckt immer lecker. Sie kann sehr gut kochen,

____

____

4. Tony fährt vorsichtiger als Bob.

____

____

5. Unsere Lehrerin änderte ihre Meinung. Wir werden heute ein Quiz veranstalten ☺

____

____

6. Die Menschen sitzen am Strand und beobachten den Sonnenuntergang.

____

____

VI. While Catherine was in Germany. She wrote an email to her parents telling them about her visit. Please write Catherine's email and write about the following points. 20 Pts.

- the food
- the weather
- Bella's friends
- a tour around Munich
- speaking German
- how much you like Germany

Anmerkung:
Mum and dad wird nur in der Anrede groß geschrieben, sonst immer klein.

Dear Mum and Dad,

Love Catherine

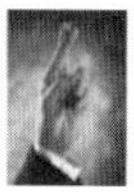

Good luck!

2.9 Schulaufgabe 4-2

Written English Test 4		**Units 1-8**
Your score ____________	**Name: ___________________**	**85 Pts.**

I. Vocabulary - Fill in the correct word in the sentences below. **25 Pts.**

1. Charlotte enjoys working with numbers. Her favourite subject is _____________ (Mathe).
2. Pop stars and actors are known by a lot of people. They are _____________ (berühmt).
3. If you 'vergleichen' two people you _____________them.
4. The Olympic Games is a a big sports _____________ (Wettbewerb).
5. An ice cream shop has got lots of different flavours of ice cream. You have to _____________ (entscheiden) which one you want.
6. The opposite of interesting is _____________ (langweilig).
7. Jim is usually late for school. I _____________ (erwarten) he will be late today.
8. The children always _____________ (sich beschweren) about school lunches. They don't like them at all and tell their mums how awful they are.
9. On Mondays I always ____________________ (sich freuen auf) the weekend because we don't have to go to school.
10. Do not cross the busy road. There are too many cars and you could get hit. It is very _____________ (gefährlich).
11. Little children often _____________ (schreien, kreischen) when they don't get what they want.
12. Never leave your _____________ (Müll) in the park. Put it in the bin or take it home with you.
13. Most school children take their lunch to school in a ______________________ (Pausenbrotbehälter).
14. We went to a _____________ (fantastisch) concert last night. The band was excellent.
15. The concert _____________ (dauern) for two and a half hours. We were tired afterwards.
16. It is important to brush your teeth twice _____________ (täglich).

17. The American English we say '_____________' (Ferien, Urlaub) and in British English we say 'holiday'.
18. A lot of models are much too _____________ (dünn). They need to eat more.
19. The school secretary works in an _____________ (Büro) on the ground floor.
20. The fans _______________ (jubeln) when their football team won the cup.
21. When you write a text in English you have to pay _____________ (Achtung) to the tenses.
22. We tried to __________________ (loswerden) the mosquitoes  in our bedroom but it didn't work.
23. The firemen _________________ (retten) the kitten that was in the tree.
24. You can go to the ________________(Bibliothek) and borrow a good book to read when you are on holiday.
25. We hope these words aren't too _______________(schwierig) for you.

II. Irregular verbs – Translate the verbs and then fill in the boxes with the form of the irregular verbs. **30 Pts.**

German	English (infinitive)	simple past	past participle
sein	1.	2.	3.
sprechen	4.	5.	6.
reiten	7.	8.	9.
tragen	10.	11.	12.
kaufen	13.	14.	15.
wachsen	16.	17.	18.
liegen	19.	20.	21.
brechen	22.	23.	24.
werfen	25.	26.	27.
stehen	28.	29.	30.

III. Grammar- in each sentence one of the words/phrases is correct. Cross out the incorrect word/phrase. 30 Pts.

1. Mary's best friend **has/have** eaten all the ice cream.
2. If you **will answer/answer** all these questions, you **will pass/pass** the test.
3. The President of America lives in the White House, **lives he? /doesn't he**?
4. The children were playing in the garden and their mum **was hanging/hung** out the washing when the storm came.
5. The **most tall/tallest** building in the city was hit by lightning.
6. We went to the zoo and saw a monkey **who's/whose** foot was broken.
7. The boy's parents didn't go **anywhere/nowhere** last weekend.
8. Our class is planning to have a bazaar next month. We **are going to/will** raise money for poor children.
9. Andrew could swim when he was three. He **was able to/was allowed to** swim ten meters.
10. Mum: 'The children are cold'.
    Dad: I **will/am going** to get their jackets'.
11. **Of** what did the neighbour's cat die **of**?
12. Have you eaten meat **which/who** was rotten?
13. Our teacher has **give/given** us four tests this year. I **have passed/passed** them all.
14. The new comedy is not **as/so** funny as the last film.
15. I **haven't spoken/didn't speak** to the director yet.
16. An armchair is more **comfortable than/comfortabler** than a hard chair.
17. There is no school this Friday. You **mustn't/don't have to** get up early.
18. Listen to that wind. There **is going to / will** be a huge storm.
19. If you tidy your room, you **will be allowed to/are allowed to** go out tonight.
20. **While/when** we were having dinner, the dog jumped up and stole my meat.
21. I **have just eaten/ just ate**. I really don't want **something/anything** to eat.
22. The young couple wants to go **somewhere /anywhere** special for dinner.
23. I think a horse runs **slower/more slowly** than a lion.
24. Chris felt **fantastically/ fantastic** when he won the race.
25. The lady **saw/have seen** the missing cat ten minutes ago.
26. The students were really happy because they **didn't have to/hadn't to** do any homework yesterday.
27. Would you like **some/any** water? You look thirsty.
28. You aren't German, **are you? / aren't you?**

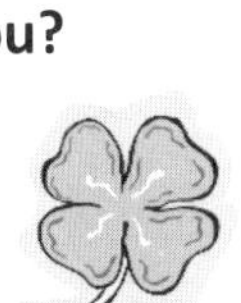

Good luck!

3 Appendix

3.1 Numbers

3.1.1 Cardinal Numbers

0	zero, oh, nought,	26	twenty – six
1	one	27	twenty – seven
2	two	28	twenty – eight
3	three	29	twenty – nine
4	four	30	thirty
5	five	40	forty
6	six	50	fifty
7	seven	60	sixty
8	eight	70	seventy
9	nine	80	eighty
10	ten	90	ninety
11	eleven	100	a/one hundred
12	twelve	101	a/one hundred and one
13	thirteen	110	a/one hundred and ten
14	fourteen	120	a hundred and twenty
15	fifteen	200	two hundred
16	sixteen	1,000	a/one thousand
17	seventeen	1,001	a thousand and one
18	eighteen	1,010	a thousand and ten
19	nineteen	2,000	two thousand
20	twenty	10,000	ten thousand
21	twenty – one	11,000	eleven thousand
22	twenty – two	100,000	a/one hundred thousand
23	twenty – three	1,000,000	a/one million
24	twenty – four	2,000,000	two million
25	twenty – five	1,000,000,000	a/one billion

Be careful:
four
fourteen
but forty.

We say 'and'
after the word
hundred.

3.1.2 Ordinal Numbers

The endings (suffixes) are: – ***st***, **– *nd*, – *rd*, or – *th***. The endings are the **last two letters of the word.**

English	short form	German	English	short form	German
fir**st**	1**st**	Erster/erstens (1.)	thi**rd**	3**rd**	Dritter/drittens
seco**nd**	2**nd**	Zweiter/zweitens	four**th**	4**th**	Vierter/viertens

English	short form	English	short form
first	1st	twentieth	20th
second	2nd	twenty – first	21st
third	3rd	twenty – second	22nd
fourth	4th	twenty – third	23rd
fifth	5th	twenty – fourth	24th
sixth	6th	twenty – fifth	25th
seventh	7th	twenty – sixth	26th
eighth	8th	twenty – seventh	27th
ninth	9th	twenty – ninth	29th
tenth	10th	thirtieth	30th
eleventh	11th	thirty – first	31st
twelfth	12th	thirty – second	32nd
twentieth	20th	one hundredth	100th
one thousandth	1,000th	one thousandth	1,000th

3.2 The Date

British English

We **write**:	10th July 2013	July 10th 2013
We **say**:	**the** tenth **of** July 2013	July **the** tenth 2013

The years before 2000 were pronounced as two numbers:
Die Jahreszahlen vor 2000 werden als zwei Zahlen ausgesprochen – das Jahrhundert und die Jahreszahl,

1869 (18) – (69) eighteen – sixty nine

1987 (19) – (87) nineteen – eighty seven

After the year 2000 (two thousand) we say the year in either of two ways:

For '2010' we say either 'two thousand ten' **or** 'twenty ten'. It is more common in Britain to use the 'twenty ten' version. ^

3.3 Prepositions

3.3.1 Prepositions of time and place

These words are ‘proper’ nouns and are always written with a **capital letter**.

Diese Wörter sind wie Eigennamen und werden **immer groß geschrieben**!

days of the week	months
Monday	January
Tuesday	February
Wednesday	March
Thursday	April
Friday	May
Saturday	June
Sunday	July
	August
	September
	October
	November
	December

3.3.2 Prepositions of Place

prepositions of place	examples	German
in	The coffee is **in** the cup.	in
on	The fork is **on** the serviette.	auf
under	The rubbish is **under** the carpet.	unter
next to/beside	The knife is **next to/beside** the plate.	neben
between	The plate is **between** the knife and fork.	zwischen
opposite	The man is **opposite** the lady.	gegenüber (von)
in front of	The cup is **in front of** the coffee pot. 	vor
behind	The coffee pot is **behind** the cup.	hinter
above	The cloud is **above** his head.	oberhalb, oben, über
below	He is **below** the cloud.	unterhalb, unter
near/close to	The little boy is **near/close to** his mum.	nahe, in der Nähe von

3.3.3 Prepositions of Direction

Prepositions of Direction are used when someone or something is moving.
We use 'to' with verbs of movement →go to, run to, walk to, fly to etc.

prepositions of direction	examples	German
to	The boy is walking **to** school.	Der Junge läuft **zur** Schule.
up	We are climbing **up** the mountain.	Wir klettern/wandern den Berg **hoch**.
down	We are climbing **down** the mountain.	Wir klettern den Berg **hinunter**.
over	The cat is jumping **over** the water.	Die Katze springt **über** das Wasser.
under	The baby is crawling **under** the table.	Das Baby krabbelt **unter** den Tisch.
through	The horse is galloping **through** the water.	Das Pferd galoppiert **durch** das Wasser.
along	She is walking **along** the road.	Sie geht die Straße **entlang**.
across	The dog is running **across** the street.	Der Hund läuft **über** die Straße.
around	The children are dancing **around** the tree.	Die Kinder tanzen **um** den Baum.
towards	The little girl is running **towards** her dad.	Das kleine Mädchen läuft ihrem Papa **entgegen**.
away from	The cat is running **away from** the dog.	Die Katze läuft **vor** dem Hund weg.
into	The cat is jumping **into** the pool.	Die Katze hüpft **in** den Pool (hinein).
on to	The boy is climbing **on to** the bed.	Der Junge klettert **auf** das Bett.
out of	The toddler is climbing **out of** the pushchair.	Das Kleinkind klettert **aus** dem Kinderwagen.
past	The bus is driving **past** the bus stop.	Der Bus fährt an der Bushaltestelle **vorbei**.

The word 'home' is an exception for prepositions of direction. We don't use a preposition of direction with 'home'. → 'home' wird **ohne** 'preposition of direction' verwendet.

Examples

- Let's go home. I am tired.
- We drove home at midnight.
- We walked home because we couldn't find a taxi.

3.3.4 Prepositions of Time

preposition of Time	examples
in	Rebecca was born **in** 2001. (year) My birthday is **in** March. (month) Children love swimming **in** summer and skiing **in** winter. (season) We have breakfast **in** the morning, cake **in** the afternoon and dinner **in** the evening.
at	My little brother goes to bed **at** 8 o'clock. (time) We celebrate with our families **at** Easter*. (religious festivals)  Hedgehogs hunt **at** night. (at night)
on	My sister's birthday is **on** 2nd September. (day) We don't have to go to school **on** Sundays. (day) Paul plays tennis **on** Friday evenings. (day)

* Easter without an 'n'. → 'eastern' with 'n' means 'östlich'.

3.3.5 A few more prepositions ...

prepositions	examples	German
at /in	The children are **at** school. (where) My father is **at** work. (where) My sister is **in** the bathroom. (room) We live **in** Germany. (country) There are a lot of nice shops **in** Oxford Street.	Die Kinder sind **in** der Schule. Mein Vater ist **in** der Arbeit. Meine Schwester ist **im** Badezimmer. Wir leben **in** Deutschland. Es gibt viele schöne Geschäfte **in** Oxford Street.
with/without	I like apple cake **with** ice cream. I eat spaghetti **without** sauce.	Ich mag Apfelkuchen **mit** Eiscreme. Ich esse Spaghetti **ohne** Sauce.
by/until	Please finish the essay **by** Friday. You can stay here **until** 5.00 pm	Bitte schreibt den Aufsatz **bis** Freitag fertig. Du kannst **bis** 17:00 Uhr hier bleiben.
during/while	We stayed indoors **during** the storm. **While** I was watching TV, the telephone rang.	Wir blieben **während** des Unwetters im Haus. **Während** wir fernsahen, klingelte das Telefon.

3.4 Opposites

English	German	opposite English	Gegenteil Deutsch
above	über	**below**	unter
before	vorher	**after**	nachher
begin	anfangen	**end**	(be –)enden
beginning	Anfang	**ending**	Ende
black	schwarz	**white**	weiß
boy	Junge	**girl**	Mädchen
brave	tapfer	**afraid**	ängstlich
brother	Bruder	**sister**	Schwester
busy	beschäftigt	**lazy**	faul
buy	kaufen	**sell**	verkaufen
ceiling	Decke	**floor**	Boden
clever	klug, clever	**stupid**	dumm
day	Tag	**night**	Nacht
dead	tot	**alive**	am Leben
delicious	lecker, köstlich	**awful**	schrecklich
easy	leicht	**difficult**	schwer
evening	Abend	**morning**	Morgen, Vormittag
far	weit	**near**	nah
first	zuerst, erster	**last**	zuletzt, letzter
forget	vergessen	**remember**	sich erinnern
full	voll	**empty**	leer
future	Zukunft	**past**	Vergangenheit
gentleman	Herr	**lady**	Dame
get off	aussteigen	**get on**	einsteigen
together	zusammen	**alone**	allein
good	gut	**bad**	schlecht
hello, hi	Hallo	**goodbye**	Tschüss
here	hier	**there**	da, dort,
hot	heiß	**cold**	kalt
hungry	hungrig	**thirsty**	durstig
late	spät	**early**	früh
long	lang	**short**	kurz
lose	verlieren	**find**	finden

English	German	opposite English	Gegenteil Deutsch
male	männlich	**female**	weiblich
man	Mann	**woman**	Frau
mother	Mutter	**father**	Vater
never	nie	**always**	immer
noisy	laut	**silent, quiet**	still, leise, ruhig
nothing	nichts	**everything**	alles
old	alt	**new**	neu
on	auf	**under**	unter
on	an	**off**	aus
open	öffnen	**close**	schließen
open	offen, geöffnet	**closed**	geschlossen, zu
outside	draußen	**inside**	drinnen
pull	ziehen	**push**	drücken
pupil	Schüler	**teacher**	Lehrer
question	Frage	**answer**	Antwort
regular	regelmäßig	**irregular**	unregelmäßig
right	rechts	**left**	links
right	richtig	**wrong**	falsch
sad	traurig	**happy**	glücklich
safe	sicher	**dangerous**	gefährlich
same	gleich	**another/different**	anders
slow	langsam	**fast**	schnell
small	klein	**big**	groß
stand up	aufstehen	**sit down**	sich hinsetzen
start	anfangen	**stop, finish**	aufhören, beenden
sugar	Zucker	**salt**	Salz
summer	Sommer	**winter**	Winter
sweet	süß	**bitter**	bitter
thin	dünn	**thick, fat**	dick
true	wahr	**false**	falsch
uncle	Onkel	**aunt**	Tante
up	herauf / hinauf	**down**	herunter
weak	schwach	**strong**	stark
yes	ja	**no**	nein
young	jung	**old**	alt

3.3 Useful Adjectives in English

Here are some useful adjectives that you can use when you write texts.

Viele Wörter haben noch viel mehr deutsche Bedeutungen, dies sind aber die gängigsten für dein Alter bzw. deine Jahrgangsstufe.

appearance	**äußeres Erscheinungsbild**	**condition**	**Zustand/Verfassung**
attractive	attraktiv, hübsch	alive	lebend
beautiful	hübsch, schön	busy	beschäftigt
big	groß	careful	vorsichtig, achtsam
bright	leuchtend	cheap	billig
clean	sauber	closed	geschlossen
clear	klar, deutlich	correct	korrekt
colourful	farbenfroh , bunt	cold	kalt
cute	süß	crazy	verrückt
dark	dunkel	dead	tot
dirty	dreckig, schmutzig	difficult	schwierig
elegant	elegant	easy	leicht
fat	dick	empty	leer
handsome	gutaussehend (nur bei Männern)	early	früh
light	hell, leicht	expensive	teuer
long	lang	famous	berühmt
plain	einfach, schlicht	free	frei /kostenlos
pretty	hübsch (for a girl)	important	wichtig
shiny	leuchtend	impossible	unmöglich
short	klein(körperlich), kurz	late	spät
skinny	dürr	lively	lebhaft, aufgeweckt
small	klein	noisy	laut
tall	groß (körperlich),	old	alt
ugly	häßlich	open	offen
		poor	arm
		quiet	leise
		real	wirklich , echt
		rich	reich
		right	korrekt, richtig, rechts
		shy	schüchtern
		sleepy	schläfrig
		strong	stark
		weak	schwach
		wrong	falsch

positive feelings	positive Gefühle	negative feelings	negative Gefühle
brave	tapfer	angry	verärgert, ärgerlich
clever	klug, clever	awful	schrecklich
comfortable	bequem, komfortabel	bad	schlecht
delicious	lecker	bored	gelangweilt
excited	aufgeregt	boring	langweilig
fair	gerecht, fair	confused	verwirrt
fantastic	fantastisch	crazy	verrückt, ausgeflippt
friendly	freundlich	cruel	grausam
funny	lustig, komisch	dangerous	gefährlich
good	gut	foolish	dumm, albern
great	toll	frightened	verängstigt
happy	glücklich	helpless	hilflos
healthy	gesund	hungry	hungrig
helpful	hilfreich, hilfsbereit	horrible	schrecklich
interesting	interessant	hurt	verletzt
jolly	fröhlich, heiter	ill	krank
kind	freundlich/liebvoll	jealous	eifersüchtig
lovely	schön, entzückend	lazy	faul
lucky	glücklich	lonely	einsam
nice	schön, nett	nasty	eklig
perfect	perfekt	naughty	böse, ungezogen
polite	höflich	nervous	nervös
proud	stolz	sad	traurig
safe	sicher	scary	unheimlich
wonderful	wunderbar	selfish	selbstsüchtig, egoistisch
		silly	dumm
		stupid	blöd, dumm
		terrible	schrecklich
		tired	müde

3.4 Useful Phrases

Now that you have learned a lot of English you may want to speak English when you go on holiday. English is very useful because you can communicate in English nearly all over the world.

Here are some useful phrases and some vocabulary that will help you when you are on holiday.

Greetings (Begrüßung)

- Hello
- Good morning
- Good afternoon
- Good evening
- Good night

Please and thank you (Danke/Bitte)

- Please. (when we ask for something)
- Thank you.
- It's a pleasure
- You're welcome
- No, thank you. (when we say 'no' to an offer)
- Yes, please. (when we say 'yes' to an offer)

Introductions (Vorstellung)

- My name is.....
- What's your name?
- Pleased to meet you
- How do you do

Asking for something (Um etwas bitten)

- I would like...
- Can I have...?
- May I have...?

Small talk

- How are you?
- Fine, thanks. How about you?
- Have a good day

If you don't understand (wenn du mal etwas nicht verstehst)

- Excuse me, Entschuldigung ...
- Sorry, Entschuldigung ...
- Can you help me? Können Sie mir helfen ...
- I'm afraid I don't understand. Leider verstehe ich nicht ...
- Can you speak more slowly? Könnten Sie bitte etwas langsamer sprechen?
- Pardon Wie bitte ...

The Flight (Flug)

You will probably fly to Britain or America. First you go to the airport, don't forget your ticket and passport. When you are at the airport you check in for your flight. Here you can also check in your luggage and decide if you would like a window or an aisle seat (Gangplatz). You get your boarding pass here.

Then you go through security where your passport and hand luggage are checked. You also go through metal detector. If you have time you can do some duty free shopping, and then go to your gate and board the plane.

When you are on the aeroplane (airplane) the flight attendant helps you find your seat. The plane takes off and you can relax and enjoy your flight. When the plane lands you will get off and go to Baggage Claim where you can get your luggage. You go through Customs and leave the airport.

Here are some useful questions/phrases for the journey. (Reise)

- Where is the check in desk, please?
  Wo ist der Check in Schalter?
- Where are the toilets?
  Wo sind die Toiletten?
- Where is Gate number 5?
  Wo ist das Gate Nummer 5?
- Is the flight on time?
  Ist der Flug pünktlich?
- I would like an orange juice, please.
  Ich hätte bitte/gerne einen Orangensaft.
- I would like to check in two bags.
  Ich möchte 2 Gepäckstücke einchecken/aufgeben.

The Hotel

When you are in London you will stay in a hotel or a bed and breakfast. You can have a single, double or twin room. You check in at reception and then go to your room. You can have breakfast in the dining room; ask for a wake – up call if you are tired. When you check out, don't forget to pay the bill.

Useful phrases for the hotel.

- We have a reservation.
  Wir haben eine Reservierung.
- What is my room number?
  Wie ist meine Zimmernummer?
- Where is the dining room?
  Wo ist der Speisesaal?
- What time is breakfast?
  Um wie viel Uhr gibt es Frühstück?
- Can I have a wake – up call at 700 am, please?
  Können Sie mich bitte um 7.00 Uhr wecken.
- Is breakfast included?
  Ist das Frühstück inbegriffen?
- I need soap, an extra pillow, an extra blanket, please.
  Ich brauche bitte noch eine Seife, ein weiteres Kissen und eine extra Decke.

Sightseeing

If you go to London you can go sightseeing. You can see Buckingham Palace, Big Ben, The London Eye, or Madame Tussauds. Make sure you have a map and a guide book so that you know where to go. Take your camera so that you can take photos. You can also buy some souvenirs to take home to Germany and show your friends. A tour guide can take you on a guided tour and show you all the tourist attractions, maybe even on an open top bus.

Useful Questions (Nützliche Fragen)

- What time does the tour begin?
  Um wie viel Uhr beginnt die Tour? / Wann beginnt die Tour?
- Where does the tour start from?
  Wo beginnt die Tour?
- How long is the tour?
  Wie lange dauert die Tour?
- Can you tell me the way to ...?
  Können Sie mir den Weg nach ... erklären?/ Können Sie mir sagen wie ich nach ... komme?
- How much does it cost to get in?
  Was kostet der Eintritt?
- What is the entrance fee?
  Was kostet der Eintritt?
- I'm lost, can you help me?
  Ich habe mich verlaufen, können Sie mir helfen?

Eating Out (auswärts essen)

When you are on holiday you will eat out. Perhaps you will go to a fast food restaurant and eat burgers and chips (french fries) or you will go to a nice restaurant. You can have a three course meal which includes starters, main course and dessert. For starters you may want soup, for your main course you may want meat (beef, lamb, pork or chicken), fish or pasta. If you order steak you have to decide if you want it rare, medium or well – done. For dessert you can have something sweet, maybe ice cream or fruit salad. You can also order something to drink (a beverage) maybe some still or sparkling water. The waiter or waitress will bring you the menu so that you can choose. After your meal you ask for the bill. Don't forget to leave a tip.

Useful questions/phrases for eating out:

- We would like a table for five, please.
  Wir möchten bitte eine Reservierung für 5 Uhr.
- Excuse me, we would like to order.
  Können wir bitte bestellen.
- Can I have the menu please?
  Kann ich bitte die Karte haben?
- For starters, I'd like a salad, please.
  Als Vorspeise hätte ich gerne einen Salat.
- I'd like a glass of coke, please.
  Ich hätte gerne ein Glas Cola.
- For the main course I'll have steak, please.
  Als Hauptgericht hätte ich gerne ein Steak.
- Can I have a side order of chips, please?
  Kann ich bitte Pommes als Beilage haben.
- Do you have any specials?
  Haben Sie eine Tageskarte?
- I'm a vegetarian.
  Ich bin Vegetarier.
- It was delicious/awful.
  Es war köstlich / schrecklich.
- Can we have the bill, please?
  Die Rechnung bitte.

3.5 False Friends and Confusing Words

There are some words that are confusing when we try to translate them. The words look the same but have a different meaning. They are called **false friends**. The words that are easy to mix up are in **bold** (**fett dargestellt**).

Hier haben wir dir ein paar Wörter zusammengestellt, die sprachlich im Englischen und Deutschen sehr ähnlich sind, aber ganz unterschiedliche Bedeutungen haben.

Some examples include:

English	German
cash **bar**	in **Bar** Kneipe
bald soon	glatzköpfig **bald**
to **become** to get	werden **bekommen**
blackboard notice board	Schultafel **Schwarzesbrett**
brave well – behaved	mutig **brav**
café coffee	Kaffeehaus **Kaffee**
chef boss	Küchenchef (Koch) **Chef**
chips (British) french fries crisps (British) **chips (American)**	**Pommes frites** Pommes frites Kartoffelchips **Kartoffelchips**
correct proper/respectable	richtig **korrekt**
director headteacher	Regisseur **Direktor** (Schuldirektor)
fast almost	schnell **fast**
floor hall	Fußboden **Flur**
handy mobile phone (British) cell phone (American)	praktisch/brauchbar **Handy**
gift poison	Geschenk **Gift**
hut hat	Hütte **Hut**
gymnasium (gym) grammar school	Turnhalle / Gymnastikraum **Gymnasium**

English	German
lemon **lime**	Zitrone Limone
marmalade **jam**	Marmelade aus Zitrusfrüchten (Orangen –) Marmelade
meaning **opinion**	Bedeutung Meinung
menu **set meal**	Speisekarte Menü
mist **manure**	feiner Nebel Mist
mustn't **needn't**	nicht dürfen nicht müssen
note **mark**	Notiz/Mitteilung Note
rent **pension**	Miete Rente
sea **lake**	Meer See
strong **strict**	stark streng
billion (1,000,000,000) **trillion (1,000,000,000,000)**	Milliarde (1.000.000.000) Billion (1.000.000.000.000)
web page	Website
where **who**	wo wer/wem/wen
while **because**	während weil
USB drive	USB stick

3.6 British English versus American English

British English	American English	German
autumn	fall	Herbst
angry	mad	böse, ärgerlich
bill	check	Rechnung
biscuit	Cookie	Keks
block of flats	apartment building	Mehrfamilienhaus
booking	reservation	Reservierung
car park	parking lot	Parkhaus /Parkplatz
chemist's	drugstore	Apotheke
chemist	pharmacist	Apotheker, Pharmazeut
chips	French fries	Pommes
cinema	movie theater	Kino
city centre	downtown	Stadtmitte, Zentrum
class	grade	Klasse
crisps	potato chips	(Kartoffel-)Chips
cooker	stove	Herd
cupboard	closet	Schrank
dressing gown	robe	Morgenmantel
film	movie	Film
fizzy drink	soda	Limonade
flat	apartment	Wohnung
football	soccer	Fußball
fortnight	two weeks	2 Wochen
full stop	period	Punkt (Grammatik)
garden	yard	Garten
ground floor	first floor	Erdgeschoss, Parterre
first floor	second floor	1. Obergeschoss
handbag	purse	Handtasche
purse	wallet/coin purse	Geldbeutel
headmaster, headmistress, head teacher	principal	Direktor / Direktorin
holiday	vacation	Urlaub
jumper	sweater	Pulli
lift	elevator	Aufzug
lorry	truck	Lastwagen

British English	American English	German
marks	grades	(Schul-)Noten
maths	math	Mathematik
motorway	highway	Autobahn
mobile phone	cellular phone (cell phone)	Handy
pavement	sidewalk	Bürgersteig
petrol	gas (gasoline)	Kraftstoff, Benzin
programme	program	Programm
trainers	sneakers	Turnschuhe
postman	mailman	Postbote
pocket money	allowance	Taschengeld
primary school	elementary school	Grundschule
queue	line	(Warte-)Schlange
rubber	eraser	Radiergummi
rubbish	trash	Abfall
rucksack	backpack	Rucksack
serviette	napkin	Serviette
sweets	candy	Süßigkeiten
shop	store	Laden
surname	last name	Nachname
term	semester	Semester, Studienhalbjahr
timetable	schedule	Stundenplan
tin	can	Dose
toilet	bathroom, restroom	Toilette
torch	flashlight	Taschenlampe
trousers	pants	Hose
tube, underground	subway	U-Bahn
zip	zipper	Reißverschluss

4 Notenschlüssel

Hier findest du verschiedene Notenschlüssel. Suche die Punktzahl, die der Gesamtpunktzahl in deiner Übungsprobe gleich bzw. am nächsten kommt. Schau dann, in welchen Punktebereich deine erreichte Punktezahl fällt in der Kopfzeile findest du dann deine erzielte Note.

Note **Gesamt-punktzahl**	**1**	**2**	**3**	**4**	**5**	**6**
24	24 – 22	21 – 19	18 – 16	15 – 12	12 – 8	7 – 0
26	26 – 24	23 – 22	21 – 18	17 – 13	13 – 10	10 – 0
28	28 – 26	25 – 23	22 – 19	18 – 15	14 – 11	10 – 0
30	30 – 27	26 – 23	23 – 19	19 – 15	15 – 11	10 – 0
32	32 – 29	28 – 25	24 – 21	20 – 16	16 – 11	10 – 0
34	34 – 31	30 – 27	26 – 23	22 – 18	17 – 12	11 – 0
36	36 – 33	32 – 29	28 – 24	24 – 18	18 – 12	11 – 0
38	38 – 35	35 – 31	30 – 25	25 – 20	19 – 14	13 – 0
40	40 – 36	35 – 31	31 – 26	26 – 20	20 – 15	14 – 0
42	42 – 38	37 – 33	32 – 28	27 – 22	21 – 15	14 – 0
46	46 – 42	41 – 36	36 – 31	29 – 23	23 – 17	16 – 0
48	48 – 43	43 – 38	37 – 32	31 – 25	24 – 17	16 – 0
50	50 – 45	44 – 39	39 – 34	33 – 26	25 – 18	17 – 0
56	56 – 51	50 – 44	43 – 37	36 – 29	28 – 20	19 – 0
60	60 – 54	53 – 47	46 – 39	38 – 31	30 – 23	22 – 0
65	65 – 59	58 – 51	50 – 42	41 – 33	32 – 24	23 – 0
70	70 – 63	62 – 55	54 – 46	45 – 36	35 – 25	24 – 0
75	75 – 67	66 – 58	57 – 48	47 – 38	37 – 27	26 – 0
80	80 – 72	71 – 62	61 – 52	51 – 41	40 – 28	27 – 0
85	85 – 77	76 – 67	66 – 56	55 – 44	43 – 30	29 – 0
90	90 – 82	81 – 71	70 – 59	58 – 46	45 – 31	30 – 0
95	95 – 86	85 – 75	74 – 62	61 – 49	48 – 33	32 – 0

5 Quellennachweis

Green Line New 2 E1 Klett Verlag 2010

Green Line New 2 E2 Klett Verlag 2010

Essential Grammar in Use (Elementary) – Raymond Murphy – Cambridge University Press 1995

Essential Grammar in Use (Intermediate) – Raymond Murphy – Cambridge University Press 1995

A Practical English Grammar – A.J. Thompson A.V. Martinet – Oxford University Press 1992

Grammar Express – Majorie Fuchs and Margaret Bonner – Pears Education Limited 2004

Understanding and Using English Grammar – Betty Schrampfer Azar – Prentice Hall Inc. 1992

Oxford Pocket Dictionary –Oxford University Press 1969

The Penguin English Reference Collection – Punctuation- The Penguin Group 1997

Eats Shoots and Leaves – Lynn Truss – Profile Books Limited 2003

First Certificate Gold -Amos Paran Addison Wesley Longman Limited 1996

www.*bbc.co.uk/worldservice/learningenglish*

www.*learnenglish.britishcouncil.org*

www.*learnenglishkids.britishcouncil.org*

www.oxforddictionaries.com

www.dictionary.cambridge.org

www.englishclub.com